T0350066

Network Data Mining
and Analysis

East China Normal University Scientific Reports
Subseries on Data Science and Engineering

ISSN: 2382-5715

Chief Editor

Weian Zheng
Changjiang Chair Professor
School of Finance and Statistics
East China Normal University, China
Email: financialmaths@gmail.com

Associate Chief Editor

Shanping Wang
Senior Editor
Journal of East China Normal University (Natural Sciences), China
Email: spwang@library.ecnu.edu.cn

This book series reports valuable research results and progress in scientific and related areas. Mainly contributed by the distinguished professors of the East China Normal University, it will cover a number of research areas in pure mathematics, financial mathematics, applied physics, computer science, environmental science, geography, estuarine and coastal science, education information technology, etc.

Published

Vol. 8   *Network Data Mining and Analysis*
        by Ming Gao (East China Normal University, China),
        Ee-Peng Lim (Singapore Management University, Singapore) and
        David Lo (Singapore Management University, Singapore)

Vol. 7   *Time-Aware Conversion Prediction for E-Commerce*
        by Wendi Ji (East China Normal University, China),
        Xiaoling Wang (East China Normal University, China) and
        Aoying Zhou (East China Normal University, China)

Vol. 6   *Discovery and Fusion of Uncertain Knowledge in Data*
        by Kun Yue (Yunnan University, China), Weiyi Liu
        (Yunnan University, China), Hao Wu (Yunnan University, China),
        Dapeng Tao (Yunnan University, China) and
        Ming Gao (East China Normal University, China)

More information on this series can also be found at https://www.worldscientific.com/series/ecnusr

(Continued at end of book)

East China Normal University Scientific Reports | **Vol. 8**

Subseries on Data Science and Engineering

Network Data Mining and Analysis

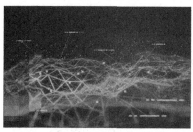

Ming Gao
East China Normal University, China

Ee-Peng Lim
Singapore Management University, Singapore

David Lo
Singapore Management University, Singapore

 **World Scientific**

NEW JERSEY · LONDON · SINGAPORE · BEIJING · SHANGHAI · HONG KONG · TAIPEI · CHENNAI · TOKYO

Published by

World Scientific Publishing Co. Pte. Ltd.

5 Toh Tuck Link, Singapore 596224

USA office: 27 Warren Street, Suite 401-402, Hackensack, NJ 07601

UK office: 57 Shelton Street, Covent Garden, London WC2H 9HE

Library of Congress Cataloging-in-Publication Data
Names: Gao, Ming (Data analyst), author. | Lo, David, author. | Lim, Ee-Peng, author.
Title: Network data mining and analysis / by Ming Gao, East China Normal University, China,
    EE-Peng Lim, Singapore Management University, Singapore,
    David Lo, Singapore Management University, Singapore.
Description: New Jersey : World Scientific, [2018] | Series: East China Normal University
    scientific reports ; volume 8 | Includes bibliographical references and index.
Identifiers: LCCN 2018033730| ISBN 9789813274952 (hc : alk. paper) |
    ISBN 9789813275973 (pbk : alk. paper)
Subjects: LCSH: Data mining.
Classification: LCC QA76.9.D343 G36 2018 | DDC 006.3/12--dc23
LC record available at https://lccn.loc.gov/2018033730

British Library Cataloguing-in-Publication Data
A catalogue record for this book is available from the British Library.

For any available supplementary material, please visit
https://www.worldscientific.com/worldscibooks/10.1142/11120#t=suppl

Desk Editors: Herbert Moses/Amanda Yun

Typeset by Stallion Press
Email: enquiries@stallionpress.com

Printed in Singapore

East China Normal University Scientific Reports

Subseries on Data Science and Engineering

Preface

The popularity of web, mobile phones and other portable devices has propelled the growth of large scale social networks such as Google$^+$, Facebook, Foursquare, and Twitter. As these online social networks become common platforms for making social connections and interactions, they also offer academic researchers a great opportunity to study social network properties at the individuals, groups, organizations and even societal levels. The research topic of social network mining is thus to investigate the interactions and relationships among users in online social networks using network properties and graph theory. Social network mining techniques have been used in a wide range of applications, such as event detection, user profiling, and user behavior analysis, etc.

Social network mining is an inherently interdisciplinary topic which involves social psychology, statistics, spectral analysis, probabilistic theory, graph theory, and others. In the beginning of this book, we summarize some basic concepts, including the types of networks, graph representations in different research communities, and the expander graphs. Based on these concepts, we will introduce the following research topics, namely:

- **Network strength measurement:** Social networks dynamically evolve as individuals join or leave, and as their interaction intensity changes over time. To characterize the strength of these large scale networks, we introduce $\mathcal{R}$-energy, a measurement for evaluating their robustness.

$\mathcal{R}$-energy not only measure the robustness of networks, but is used to detect events and regular trend patterns that affect network robustness.

- **Network linkage:** The popularity of social media has led many individuals to creating accounts in different online social networks. Network linkage refers to linking different accounts from different social network that belongs to the unique user. Identifying these multiple accounts belonging to same user is of critical importance to user profiling, community detection, user behavior understanding, and product recommendation. In this book, we propose an unsupervised learning framework to find the same individuals across heterogeneous social networks.

- **Quasi-biclique community detection:** Bipartite graph is a very important graph model in many real world applications, which involve product, movie or music ratings. Detecting dense sub-structures in bipartite graphs help us understand user behaviors so as to perform personalized recommendations. Comparing to detecting bicliques from a bipartite graph, we define a dense subgraph called quasi-biclique community (QBC), which permits some missing edges between inter-set vertices, and propose an efficient algorithm to detect all maximal $QBCs$ from a bipartite graph.

- **Quasi-antagonistic community detection:** Many of today's social networks are signed graphs with positive and negative links, where the positive links represent friendship or trust while the negative links represent foe or distrust. Based on the social balanced theory, we define a new dense local structure in a signed graph, namely quasi-antagonistic community (QAC). We develop a novel algorithm called MASCOT to efficiently detect all $MQACs$ in a signed graph.

Ming Gao, Ee-Peng Lim, and David Lo
December, 2017

About the Authors

 **Ming Gao** is an Associate Professor of School of Data Science and Engineering in East China Normal University. He received his Ph.D. from Fudan University, China. Prior to joining ECNU, he worked as a Postdoctoral Fellow of the Living Analytics Research Center (LARC), Singapore Management University. His main research interests include user profiling, social mining, knowledge graph, and computing education. He served as a co-chair of the 1st International IEEE ICBK Workshop on Analyzing and Predicting Interaction Behaviors.

 **Ee-Peng Lim** is the Director of the Living Analytics Research Center (LARC) and a Professor of Information Systems in the Singapore Management University. He received his Ph.D. from the University of Minnesota. His research interests include social media mining, smart cities, and information integration. He is currently an Associate Editor of the *ACM Transactions on the Web* (*TWeb*), *IEEE Transactions on Knowledge and Data Engineering* (*TKDE*), and few others journals. He is the Conference Co-Chair of CIKM2017 and serves on the Steering Committee of the International

Conference on Asian Digital Libraries (ICADL), Pacific Asia Conference on Knowledge Discovery and Data Mining (PAKDD), and International Conference on Social Informatics (Socinfo).

 **David Lo** is an Associate Professor of Information Systems in the Singapore Management University. He received his Ph.D. from the National University of Singapore. His research interests include social media mining, software engineering, and cybersecurity. He is an editorial board member of *Information Systems*, *Empirical Software Engineering*, and a few other journals. He was the General Chair of the 31st IEEE/ACM International Conference on Automated Software Engineering (ASE16) and serves (or has served) on the Steering Committee of ASE, IEEE International Conference on Software Analysis, Evolution and Reengineering, and IEEE Working Conference on Source Code Analysis and Manipulation.

Acknowledgments

In the first place, I would like to express my sincere gratitude to my collaborators Prof. Ee-Peng Lim and Prof. David Lo for providing guidance and freedom to pursue my social network mining research when I worked as a research fellow at the Living Analytics Research Centre (LARC) of School of Information Systems in Singapore Management University. We had many extremely interesting and stimulating discussions which leads to the series of research works covered in this book. I would also like to thank all my colleagues, including Prof. Feida Zhu, Philips Kokoh Prasetyo, Bing Tian Dai, Richard Jayadi Oentaryo, and Freddy Chong Tat Chua for all their helps and comments.

I would also like to specially thank Prof. Aoying Zhou for encouraging and supporting me to publish this book. Without his high scholarly opinions on the topics, this book may not have been written. I would like to thank the Ph.D. students at East China Normal University, namely Yingnan Fu, for organizing the book manuscript.

Finally, I would like to thank my wife Haiping Yu for being my tower of strength, supporting my research career throughout including writing this book. She does a wonderful job looking after our family and raising our lovely son, Yichen Gao. I shall therefore dedicate this book to my wife and son. I am indebted to them for not spending enough time with them due to my work. I would like to thank my parents, parents-in-law, and sisters for allowing me to follow my ambitions including the years I spent in Singapore.

This book has been supported by the National Key Research and Development Program of China under Grant No. 2016YFB1000905. This book is also supported by the National Research Foundation, Prime Ministers Office, Singapore under its International Research Centres in Singapore Funding Initiative. This book is also supported by the NSFC under Grant Nos. U1401256, 61672234, 61502236, and 61472321. This book is also supported by the Shanghai Agriculture Applied Technology Development Program, China (Grant No. T20170303).

Ming Gao

Contents

Chapter 1

Introduction to Social Networks

In recent years, with the development of Internet technology, online social networks have gradually changed people's lives. Facebook, Twitter, Sina Weibo, etc., have become more and more popular. So far, there are more than 2.2 billion and 500 million registered users on Facebook and Twitter, respectively. Every day, hundreds of millions of people spend a lot of time on the social network platforms to share, communicate, connect, interact, and create massive information, which has directly contributed to the arrival of the era of big data. Large amounts of data is generated in the online social networks, including users' sharing, relationships, and interactions, etc. These data provides an opportunity for us to learn about the patterns of interaction between users, to detect network events, and to predict user behaviors. Thus, massive social network data has great research value and huge market applications. Social network mining, which is a new research field with rapid growth, has become a hot research topic. In this research area, social connections are important and inseparable features of social networks. Compared with traditional data mining, we need some new methodologies to analyze and mine the social network data which are related to the social psychology, statistics, spectral analysis, probabilistic theory, graph theory, and graph mining, and so on.

1.1 Social Networks

A social network consists of a set of social actors, a set of social relationships, and other social interactions between actors. With the rapid development of Internet technology, there have been a large number of social platforms, such as Facebook, Twitter, Sina Weibo, YouTube, etc. These social platforms have worked as social sensors to sense users'

1

behaviors. Every day billions of people spend a lot of time communicating on social platforms, thus generating a lot of user behavior data. These data form an online social network.

Nowadays, online social networks have become important channels for people to obtain and spread information, to make friends, and as the sources of entertainment. Because of the complexity of social network structures and the massive information, it is also a frontier research field in computational science, management science, psychology science, behavior science, and sociology. As a result, the analysis and mining of social networks have already influenced the political, economic, and culture development of countries. It has played an increasingly important role in the field of business intelligence, social management, academic research, and certain other fields.

Through social network mining, we can analyze the users' behaviors and preferences to help businesses recommend products better. Sitaram Asur of HP Labs has succeeded in predicting the movie's box office by analyzing Twitter data (Asur and Huberman, 2010). Analysis of user location data can help policemen to find users with abnormal behaviors, and thus maintain law and order. We can effectively mobilize public opinion for monitoring and eliminate negative social network information through a study of social network information dissemination. Real-time analysis of network robustness also allows us to detect the internal and external events in the social networks. In Tunisia and Egypt, the governments' opponents have used social networks for revolutionary propaganda, making a seemingly powerful regime collapse in half a month. Therefore, online social network research has been of significant concern at home and abroad in recent years.

At present, the main research objectives of social network mining are as follows:

(1) Analysis of the topological characteristics of social networks.
(2) User behavior analysis.
(3) Socialization recommendation.
(4) Community detection.
(5) Information dissemination in social networks.

1.2 Challenges of Social Network Mining

Social network mining has attracted the attentions of both academia and industry, and it has produced many research results. However, social network mining is still in its infancy. With the development of online social networks, social network mining has been facing the following challenges:

Large scale: Social networks are usually large-scale networks with millions of vertices, which are complex and have massive amounts of data. But most of the existing representative methods are only tested on small-scale social networks, and thus the scalability of these methods is poor. Therefore, how to design an accurate and scalable method is a problem that needs to be solved.

Heterogeneity: Data heterogeneity is a great challenge in social network mining. User attributes and behaviors can differ vastly across social networks due to the different site designs. In many situations, we need to incorporate the heterogeneous user behaviors to build a reasonable model. It is a natural question how to model the heterogeneous user behaviors.

Uncertainty: The same users may provide inconsistent information for the same attribute in different social networks. This could be due to the input errors or users' intentional omission. These situations often need a combination of natural language processing, machine learning, data mining, and some other technologies to help deal with them, which thus poses the challenges of user behavior mining and analysis.

Mutual influence: In many traditional problems, research objects are treated as the independent entities. However, individuals in social networks are connected to one another, and their behaviors also impact each other. Social network has the power to dramatically influence our choices, actions, thoughts, feelings, even our desires. In social network-related researches, we cannot analyze and mine user behaviors independently.

Fragmented data: Today's information-based dynamic platforms provide a convenient way for users to soak in numerous accounts of different online social networks simultaneously. Moreover, user behaviors are usually fragmented, with uncertainty, incompleteness, and varying levels of quality. This fragmented data brings many challenges to us since each piece provides some limited information, but not the whole picture.

1.3 Chapter Organization

The rest of this book organized as follows. In Chapter 2, we introduced some basic concepts of network modeling. In Chapter 3, we develop $\mathcal{R}$-energy as a new metric of network robustness based on the spectral analysis of network structures. In Chapter 4, we propose an unsupervised method, Collective Network Linkage, to link users across heterogeneous social networks. In Chapters 5 and 6, we detect dense sub-structures from bipartite graphs and signed graphs.

Chapter 2

Network Modeling

We live in a connected world. The transportation network has made travel much more convenient; the financial network has made people's consumption and financial management very easy; and communication networks have helped spread information very quickly. Network brings people's lives closer and promotes the development of industries rapidly. These connected networks can be represented by the different graphs. The information form networks can help us to predict connections, make user portraits, recommend production, etc. In this chapter, we will introduce some basic concepts about graphs in network mining.

2.1 The Types of Networks

In a network, every individual can be represented as a vertex (node) of a graph, and two individuals who interact each other can be connected with an edge in the graph. Social networks may be represented as many different types of graphs.

2.1.1 Graph

In this section, we list some common notations used in this book.

Definition 2.1 (Graph). A **graph** G is a binary tuple, denoted as $G = (V, E)$, where V is the vertex set, and $E \subset V \times V$ is the edge set.

Graph represents the friendships between individuals (users, people, etc.), which are modeled as or vertices, and the connection or relationship between two vertices is called an edge. In some social platforms, we may care about the directions of relationships. For example, Twitter promotes two-way communication with its following and follower friends, it does not force a connection between them, i.e., you can follow an account, but it does not have to follow you, and vice versa. Furthermore, we distinguish the graphs as directed and undirected graphs. This is described below.

Definition 2.2 (Directed and Undirected Graphs). Given a graph $G = (V, E)$,

(1) graph G is a **directed graph** if $\exists i \neq j \in \{1, 2, \dots, |V|\}$ such that $(v_i, v_j) \in E$, but $(v_j, v_i) \notin E$;
(2) graph G is an **undirected graph**, for $1 \leq i \neq j \leq |V|$, if $(v_i, v_j) \in E$, we have $(v_j, v_i) \in E$.

In some cases, we may care about the strength of a relationship between two vertices. For example, if two individuals contact frequently in a communication network, it indicates that a strong and stable relationship may form between them. The following definition of weighted graph can be employed to capture the strength of relationships in a graph.

Definition 2.3 (Weighted Graph). Given a vertex set V, an edge set E, and a weight matrix W, a triple $G = (V, E, W)$ represents a **weighted graph**, where W_{ij} denotes the strength of edge $e_{ij} \in E$ from nodes v_i to v_j.

To save the space for storage a graph, a weighted graph can be treated as a binary tuple $G = (V, W)$, where $W_{ij} = 0$ means there is no relationship between vertices v_i and v_j, otherwise W_{ij} represents the strength of edge e_{ij}. In addition, $W_{ij} = W_{ji}$ for all i and j if the graph is an undirected one.

In practice, there are many applications which can be modeled as weighted graphs. An example is the interaction graph, which is a way of representing how individuals are connected by a social network. In general, an interaction graph is a directed graph in which vertices represent users in the social platform and edge weights represent strength of interactions between two individuals. Another example is the transportation network, which is a way of representing the stream of people and business logistics, where each vertex denotes an airport (a transfer station, warehouse, etc.)

and an edge weight is the number of flights (trains, heavy trucks, etc.) between two airports (a transfer station, warehouse, etc.) during a period.

An individual in a graph may be more important if he/she connects to many others, which can be modeled as neighbor and degree of the individual.

Definition 2.4 (Neighbor and Degree). Given a graph $G = (V, E)$, for $\forall v \in V$, it's **neighbor** and **degree** can be defined as

$$N(v) = \{u|(v, u) \in E\} \quad \text{and} \quad d(v) = |N(v)|.$$

Degree $d(v)$ is the number of elements in $N(v)$, which is defined as the set of neighbors of vertex v. In a directed graph, there are in-degrees and out-degrees for a vertex, which are defined as follows:

$$d(v)^{\text{out}} = |\{u|(v, u) \in E\}|,$$

$$d(v)^{\text{in}} = |\{u|(u, v) \in E\}|.$$

Note that $d(v)^{\text{out}}$ is identical to $d(v)^{\text{in}}$ for all vertices in an undirected graph. Similarly, for a vertex v in an undirected and weighted graph, it's degree can be defined as

$$d(v) = \sum_{u \in V} W_{vu}.$$

In addition, there are some special graphs in the real world, such as the following defined regular graph:

Definition 2.5 (Regular Graph). A **regular graph** is a graph where each vertex has the same number of neighbors. Specially, a k-**regular graph** is a regular graph, where each vertex has the same k neighbors.

Figure 2.1 shows k-regular graph when $k = 1, 2$, and 3. Note that k is not larger than $|V| - 1$ since each vertex has at most $|V| - 1$ neighbors in a given graph $G = (V, E)$. Therefore, we define a special k-regular graph when $k = |V| - 1$.

Definition 2.6 (Complete Graph). Given a graph $G = (V, E)$, graph G is a **complete graph** if every pair of vertices from V are connected. Note that a complete graph is also called a **clique**.

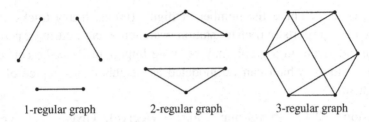

1-regular graph   2-regular graph   3-regular graph

Fig. 2.1: k-regular graph with $k = 1$, 2, and 3.

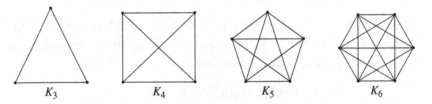

K_3 K_4 K_5 K_6

Fig. 2.2: Complete graph K_n with $n = 3$, 4, 5, and 6.

That is, graph $G = (V, E)$ is a complete graph if $\deg(v) = |V| - 1$ for $\forall v \in V$, i.e., each vertex in the graph has exactly $|V| - 1$ neighbors. Figure 2.2 illustrate four complete graphs with 3, 4, 5, and 6 vertices. Obviously, a complete graph is the densest graph made up of the given vertex set V.

2.1.2 Signed Graph

A **signed graph** is a special case of the weighted graph, which edges have binary weights or labels, namely positive (+ or 1) and negative (− or −1). In the real world, there are many defined signed graphs for modeling the trust and distrust relationships between vertices.

Definition 2.7 (Signed Graph). A **signed graph** G is a triple (V, E^+, E^-), where V is the vertex set, and E^+ and E^- represent the positive and negative edge sets, respectively.

As shown in Figure 2.3, G is a signed graph, where $V = \{v_1, v_2, v_3\}$, $E^+ = \{(v_1, v_2), (v_1, v_3), (v_2, v_1), (v_3, v_1)\}$, and $E^- = \{(v_3, v_2), (v_2, v_3)\}$. That is, users v_1 and v_2 are friends, but v_2 and v_3 are foes. For example,

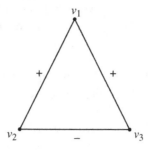

Fig. 2.3: A signed graph $G = (V, E^+, E^-)$.

there are two political fractions (e.g., republicans vs. democrats) in a politician community, supporters of two rival product brands (e.g., Apple vs. Samsung) in the business domain, or fans of two competing artists (e.g., Justin Bieber vs. Conor Maynard[1]) in the entertainment circle.

In a signed graph, both positive-degree and negative-degree for a vertex can exist, which are defined as follows:

$$d(v)^+ = |\{u|(v, u) \in E^+\}|,$$

$$d(v)^- = |\{u|(v, u) \in E^-\}|.$$

Therefore, for the signed graph shown in Figure 2.3, we have $d(v_1)^+ = 2$, $d(v_2)^+ = 1$, $d(v_2)^- = 1$, and $d(v_3)^- = 1$.

2.1.3 *Bipartite Graph*

In previous graph definitions, all members of vertex sets are the same type of objects. However, there are many applications where different objects can be divided into two or more disjoint non-empty sets. For example, researchers publish papers in some conferences or journals. In this case, one set consists of researchers, and the other one consists of papers published by them. If a researcher is a coauthor of a paper, a link forms to connect the researcher and the paper. Many examples, such as

---

[1]Justin Bieber and Conor Maynard are two teens who enjoy wide success in their singing career.

item adoption, music listening, APP downloading, book reading, etc., can be considered as similar cases. We model these cases as bipartite graphs.

Definition 2.8 (Bipartite Graph). A **bipartite graph** G is a triple (V, U, E), where V and U are two vertex sets with $V \cap U = \emptyset$, and

$$E = \{(v, u) \quad \text{or} \quad (u, v) | v \in V, u \in U\}.$$

A bipartite graph $G(V, E)$ is a graph where the involved objects can be grouped into two disjoint sets; for all edges, one endpoint is in one set and the other endpoint is in the other set, i.e., every edge connects inter-set vertices, but there does not exist an edge to connect the intra-set vertices. For example, Figure 2.4 demonstrates a bipartite graph. In the graph, V and U are two disjoint vertex sets, and all edges connect vertices from both sets V and U.

In many applications, we aim at detecting some dense subgraphs from a bipartite graph, such as bicliques.

Definition 2.9 (Biclique). Given a bipartite graph $G = (V, U, E)$, graph G is a **biclique** if $\forall v \in V$ and $\forall u \in U$, we have both $(v, u) \in E$ and $(u, v) \in E$.

That is, graph $G = (V, U, E)$ is a biclique if each vertex in V has $|U|$ neighbors in set U, and each vertex in U has $|V|$ neighbors in set V. Figure 2.5 illustrate a biclique. Obviously, a biclique is the densest graph between vertex sets V and U.

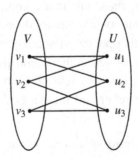

Fig. 2.4: A bipartite graph $G = (V, U, E)$.

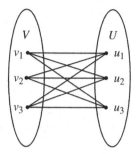

Fig. 2.5: A biclique $G = (V, U, E)$.

2.2 Network Modeling

In the previous section, we defined some types of graphs. However, it is still a problem to represent graphs for a computer. In this section, we will introduce some approaches to do that.

2.2.1 *Adjacency Matrix*

A simple way of modeling a graph is to use the adjacency matrix, which can be defined as follows.

Definition 2.10 (Adjacency Matrix). Given a **graph** $G = (V, E)$, the **adjacency matrix** of graph G is a $\mathcal{R}^{|V| \times |V|}$ matrix, denoted as A_G, its' entries can be defined as

$$A_G(i, j) := \begin{cases} 1, & \text{if } (v_i, v_j) \in E; \\ 0, & \text{otherwise.} \end{cases} \quad (2.1)$$

Let $d(v_i)$ be the degree of vertex $v_i \in E$, it can be computed as $d(v_i) = \sum_{j \neq i} A_G(i, j)$. **Degree matrix** D_G can be defined as

$$D_G(i, j) := \begin{cases} d(v_i), & \text{if } i = j \text{ and } v_i \in V; \\ 0, & \text{otherwise.} \end{cases} \quad (2.2)$$

Adjacency matrix A_G represents the relationships between the adjacent vertices. If there is an edge between two vertices, the corresponding element in the matrix is 1, otherwise it is 0.

Example 2.1. Figure 2.6 shows two directed and undirected graphs with four vertices, the adjacency matrices of the graphs in Figure 2.6 can be

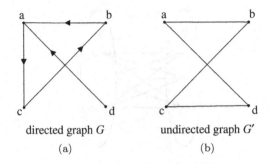

directed graph G undirected graph G'

(a)   (b)

Fig. 2.6: Directed and undirected graphs.

listed as

$$A_G = \begin{pmatrix} 0 & 0 & 1 & 0 \\ 1 & 0 & 0 & 0 \\ 0 & 1 & 0 & 0 \\ 1 & 0 & 0 & 0 \end{pmatrix}, \quad A_{G'} = \begin{pmatrix} 0 & 1 & 0 & 1 \\ 1 & 0 & 1 & 0 \\ 0 & 1 & 0 & 1 \\ 1 & 0 & 1 & 0 \end{pmatrix}$$

Property.

(1) Adjacency matrix A_G of graph G is a symmetric matrix if the graph is an undirected graph.
(2) Given a directed graph $G = (V, E)$, let A_G be its adjacency matrix, then we have

$$d(v_i)^{\text{out}} = \sum_{j=1}^{|V|} A_G(i, j);$$

$$d(v_i)^{\text{in}} = \sum_{j=1}^{|V|} A_G(j, i).$$

In terms of the adjacency matrices A_G and $A_{G'}$, we can conclude that graphs G and G' are directed and undirected graphs, respectively.

2.2.2 *Random Walk*

Given a graph and a starting vertex, a walker moves to one of its neighbors with the probability that is proportional to the weight of the edge linking them. The random sequence of vertices selected this way is a random walk on the graph.

Definition 2.11 (Transition Probability Matrix). Given a graph $G = (V, E)$ and adjacency matrix A_G, P_G is the **transition probability matrix** of the random walk on graph G, where each entry of P_G is defined as

$$P_G(i, j) := \begin{cases} \dfrac{1}{d(v_i)}, & \text{if } (v_i, v_j) \in E; \\ 0, & \text{otherwise.} \end{cases} \tag{2.3}$$

Similarly, transition probability matrix P_G of the random walk on a weighted graph G can be defined as

$$P_G(i, j) := \frac{W_{i,j}}{d(v_i)}.$$

Example 2.2. Given two directed and undirected graphs in Figure 2.6, the transition probability matrices of graphs in Figure 2.6 can be computed as

$$P_G = \begin{pmatrix} 0 & 0 & 1 & 0 \\ 1 & 0 & 0 & 0 \\ 0 & 1 & 0 & 0 \\ 1 & 0 & 0 & 0 \end{pmatrix}, \quad P_{G'} = \begin{pmatrix} 0 & \frac{1}{2} & 0 & \frac{1}{2} \\ \frac{1}{2} & 0 & \frac{1}{2} & 0 \\ 0 & \frac{1}{2} & 0 & \frac{1}{2} \\ \frac{1}{2} & 0 & \frac{1}{2} & 0 \end{pmatrix}.$$

Hence, we can use the random walk to model a graph.

2.2.3 *Laplacian Matrix*

The Laplacian matrix, sometimes called admittance matrix or discrete Laplacian, is a matrix representation of a graph. The Laplacian matrix can be used to find many useful properties of a graph.

Definition 2.12 (Laplacian Matrix). Given a graph $G = (V, E)$, it's Laplacian matrix L_G is defined as

$$L_G = D_G - A_G, \tag{2.4}$$

where D_G and A_G are the degree and adjacency matrices of G (Chung, 1997).

Example 2.3. Given the undirected graph in Figure 2.6(b), the degree matrix D_G of the graph is as follows:

$$D_G = \begin{pmatrix} 2 & 0 & 0 & 0 \\ 0 & 2 & 0 & 0 \\ 0 & 0 & 2 & 0 \\ 0 & 0 & 0 & 2 \end{pmatrix}.$$

Therefore, we can compute Laplacian matrix L_G of the graph,

$$L_G = \begin{pmatrix} 2 & -1 & 0 & -1 \\ -1 & 2 & -1 & 0 \\ 0 & -1 & 2 & -1 \\ -1 & 0 & -1 & 2 \end{pmatrix}.$$

In addition, the elements of L_G are also given by

$$L_G(i, j) = \begin{cases} \deg(v_i), & \text{if } i = j; \\ -1, & \text{if } i \neq j \text{ and } v_i \text{ is adjacent to } v_j; \\ 0, & \text{otherwise.} \end{cases} \tag{2.5}$$

Property.

(1) L_G is a positive semidefinite matrix if G is an undirected graph;
(2) The minimum eigenvalue of L_G is 0, and the corresponding eigenvector is $\overrightarrow{1}$, i.e., let λ_i be the eigenvalue of L_G, then $0 = \lambda_1 \leq \lambda_2 \leq \cdots \leq \lambda_n$.

2.2.4 *Normalized Laplacian Matrix*

Consider an undirected graph $G = (V, E)$ with vertex set V and edge set E. Let A_G and D_G denote the adjacency and degree matrices of graph G. Now we define the **normalized Laplacian matrix**.

Definition 2.13 (Normalized Laplacian Matrix). Normalized Laplacian matrix N_G of a graph G with non-negative adjacency matrix A_G is given by

$$N_G := I - D_G^{-1/2} A_G D_G^{-1/2}.$$

We denote

$$0 = \zeta_1 \leq \zeta_2 \leq \cdots \leq \zeta_n \qquad (2.6)$$

as the eigenvalues of normalized Laplacian matrix N_G.

The elements of N_G are also given by

$$N_G(i, j) = \begin{cases} 1, & \text{if } i = j; \\ -\dfrac{1}{\sqrt{\deg(v_i)\deg(v_j)}}, & \text{if } i \neq j \text{ and } v_i \text{ is adjacent to } v_j; \\ 0, & \text{otherwise.} \end{cases} \qquad (2.7)$$

Example 2.4. The normalized Laplacian matrix of the undirected graph in Figure 2.6(b) can be computed as

$$N_G = \begin{pmatrix} 1 & -\frac{1}{2} & 0 & -\frac{1}{2} \\ -\frac{1}{2} & 1 & -\frac{1}{2} & 0 \\ 0 & -\frac{1}{2} & 1 & -\frac{1}{2} \\ -\frac{1}{2} & 0 & -\frac{1}{2} & 1 \end{pmatrix}.$$

There are several important properties regarding the eigenvalues of normalized Laplacian matrix as follows.

Property. The eigenvalues of the normalized Laplacian matrix of a graph with n vertices satisfy the following properties:

(1) Let ζ_i be the eigenvalues of normalized Laplacian matrix N_G, then $\zeta_i \geq 0$;
(2) N_G is also a positive semidefinite matrix if G is an undirected graph;
(3) Normalized Laplacian matrix N_G is a symmetric matrix if graph G is an undirected graph.

Since both L_G and N_G of an undirected graph are symmetric matrices, they make it convenient for us to analyze and mine graphs. However, the transition probability matrix of a graph may not be a symmetric matrix, even if it is an undirected graph.

2.3 Topological Structure

2.3.1 *Balanced Theory*

Social balance theory, also called structural balance theory, discusses the consistency of individual relationships. In social networks, the triangular relationship is one of the most basic group structures. The social balance theory can be described as "the friend of my friend is my friend" (Heider, 2013). We demonstrate all triangles in a signed graph in Figure 2.7.

In Figure 2.7, positive and negative edges represent friends and foes, respectively. Let w_{ij} denote the weight of the edge between v_i and v_j. We assume that weight $w_{ij} = 1$ if it is a positive edge, and $w_{ij} = -1$ if it is a negative edge. For three vertices a, b, and c of a triangle, the triangle is stable if and only if it satisfies $w_{ab}w_{ac}w_{bc} = 1$. According to the above statement, we can see that triangles in Figures 2.7(a)–2.7(d) are balanced, and triangles in Figures 2.7(e)–2.7(h) are unbalanced. An unbalanced triangle is unstable and will eventually change into a balanced triangle.

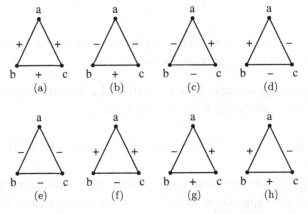

Fig. 2.7: All cases of triangles in a signed graph of three vertices.

2.3.2 *Robustness*

Robustness is the key to evaluate the system survivability in abnormal and dangerous situations. In this section, we introduce some existing metrics for evaluating the network robustness.

2.3.2.1 *Connectivity Robustness*

Given graph $G = (V, E)$, where V is the vertex set and E is the edge set, there are three metrics to evaluate the connectivity of a graph.

Definition 2.14 (Node Connectivity). **Node connectivity** $\upsilon(G)$ of connected graph G is the smallest number of nodes whose removal results in a disconnected or single-node graph (Dekker and Colbert, 2004).

Node connectivity of a graph may be defined by the number of vertices that may be removed to break the graphs into multiple connected components.

Definition 2.15 (Edge Connectivity). **Edge connectivity** $\varepsilon(G)$ of connected graph G is the smallest number of edges whose removal results in a disconnected graph (Dekker and Colbert, 2004).

Edge connectivity of a graph may be defined by the number of edges that may be removed to break the graphs into multiple connected components.

Definition 2.16 (Algebraic Connectivity). Let L be the Laplacian matrix of G, **algebraic connectivity** $\lambda(G)$ of G is the second smallest eigenvalue of L (Jamakovic and Van Mieghem, 2008).

Node, edge, and algebraic connectivity all reflect how well connected the graph is. A larger connectivity value suggests that a graph is more robust.

Example 2.5. Figures 2.8(a) and 2.8(b) show two undirected graphs with five vertices.

In Figure 2.8(a), if we remove two vertices or two edges, the graph will become a disconnected graph. So, the node connectivity and the edge connectivity are two. Similarly, we can see the node and edge connectivity of the graph in Figure 2.8(b) are also two.

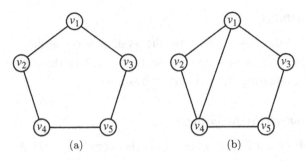

Fig. 2.8: Two graphs.

Table 2.1: Connectivity robustness metrics for graphs in Figure 2.8.

| Graph | Connectivity | | |
	Node	Edge	Algebraic
Figure 2.8(a)	2	2	1.382
Figure 2.8(b)	2	2	1.382

For the graphs in Figure 2.8, their Laplacian matrices are as follows:

$$P = \begin{pmatrix} 2 & -1 & -1 & 0 & 0 \\ -1 & 2 & 0 & -1 & 0 \\ -1 & 0 & 2 & 0 & -1 \\ 0 & -1 & 0 & 2 & -1 \\ 0 & 0 & -1 & -1 & 2 \end{pmatrix}, \quad Q = \begin{pmatrix} 3 & -1 & -1 & -1 & 0 \\ -1 & 2 & 0 & -1 & 0 \\ -1 & 0 & 2 & 0 & -1 \\ -1 & -1 & 0 & 3 & -1 \\ 0 & 0 & -1 & -1 & 2 \end{pmatrix}.$$

We can compute that the second smallest eigenvalues of these (i.e., the algebraic connectivity) are all 1.382. The node, edge, and algebraic connectivity of Figure 2.8 are shown in Table 2.1.

Remark 2.1.

(1) Algebraic connectivity is closely related to node connectivity and edge connectivity by the following inequality: $\lambda(G) \leq \upsilon(G) \leq \varepsilon(G)$ (Fiedler, 1973).

(2) These metrics are only applicable to connected graphs. Even though a highly robust giant component exists in a disconnected graph with

very few connected components, the graph is considered not robust at all as all these measures return zero values.

(3) They quantify robustness using specific (optimal) combinations of vertices (for node connectivity), specific combination of edges (for edge connectivity), and specific eigenvalue (for algebraic connectivity). For example, the network in Figure 2.8(b) is intuitively more robust than another network in Figure 2.8(a). However, the node, edge, and algebraic connectivity in Table 2.1 show that the robustness of the two networks are the same.

2.3.2.2 Expansion Robustness

An **expander graph** is a sparse graph which has strong connectivity properties. It is a graph in which every subset of the vertex set may not be too large, but has a large boundary. The goodness (or robustness) of the expander graph can be measured by **vertex expansion**, **edge expansion**, and **Cheeger constant**. Let $G = (V, E)$ be a connected and undirected graph. For $S, T \subset V$, $E(S, T)$ denotes the set of inter-set edges from S to T, i.e.,

$$E(S, T) = \{(u, v) | u \in S, v \in T, (u, v) \in E\}.$$

Definition 2.17 (Boundary). Let $G = (V, E)$ be a graph, given a set $S \subset V$,

(1) the **outer vertex boundary** (Bobkov *et al.*, 2000), denoted as $\partial_{\text{out}}(S)$, is the set of vertices in $\overline{S}$ with at least one neighbor in S, that is,

$$\partial_{\text{out}}(S) = \{u | u \in \overline{S}, \exists v \in S, \text{ s.t., } (v, u) \in E\};$$

(2) the **edge boundary** (Hoory *et al.*, 2006), denoted as $\partial(S)$, is $\partial(S) = E(S, \overline{S})$. This is the set of edges emanating from set S to its complement,

$$\partial(S) = \{(v, u) | v \in S, u \in \overline{S}, \text{ s.t., } (v, u) \in E\}.$$

Definition 2.18 (Expansion). Let $G = (V, E)$ be a graph,

(1) The **vertex expansion** (Bobkov *et al.*, 2000) of graph G, denoted as $h_v(G)$, is defined as

$$h_v(G) = \min_{S \subset V, 0 < |S| \le \frac{|V|}{2}} \frac{|\partial_{\text{out}}(S)|}{|S|}. \tag{2.8}$$

(2) The **edge expansion** (Hoory *et al.*, 2006) of graph G, denoted as $h_e(G)$, is defined as

$$h_e(G) = \min_{S \subset V, 0 < |S| \le \frac{|V|}{2}} \frac{|\partial(S)|}{|S|}. \tag{2.9}$$

Therefore, every connected graph is an expander; however, different connected graphs have different expansion measurements. The complete graph has the best expansion property. However, disconnected graphs are not expanders since both vertex expansion and edge expansion of a connected component are 0 if the graph is a disconnected graph.

Definition 2.19 (Cheeger Constant). The **Cheeger constant** (Alvey, 2011) of graph G, denoted $h(G)$, is defined as

$$h(G) = \inf_{S \subset V} \frac{|\partial(S)|}{\min\{|S|, |\overline{S}|\}}. \tag{2.10}$$

The vertex expansion, edge expansion, and Cheeger constant can be used to measure the robustness of graphs. By comparing their difference, we can figure out how well connected the graph is. The larger the expansion measurement is, the more robust a graph is.

Example 2.6. Consider all cuts of the graphs shown in Figures 2.8(a) and 2.8(b), we can see the vertex expansion, edge expansion, and Cheeger constant in Table 2.2. These metrics indicate that the two graphs shown in Figures 2.8 have identical robustness measurements.

Remark 2.2.

(1) Cheeger constant $h(G)$ is related to $\lambda_1(G)$ (the smallest eigenvalue of the Laplacian matrix of graph G), by the following inequality: $\lambda_1(G) \ge \frac{h^2(G)}{4}$ (Alvey, 2011).

Table 2.2: Expansion metrics for graphs in Figure 2.8.

Graph	Expansion		
	Vertex	Edge	Cheeger
Figure 2.8(a)	1	1	0.5
Figure 2.8(b)	1	1	0.5

(2) These metrics may not tell the truth about the graph robustness. From Table 2.2, we can observe that the vertex expansion, edge expansion, and Cheeger constant of graphs shown in Figures 2.8(a) and 2.8(b) are the same, but the graph in Figure 2.8(b) is more robust than that in Figure 2.8(a) intuitively.

(3) They are difficult to scale up to the large graphs with millions of vertices and edges. Even though these metrics tell us the truth about the graph robustness, it is computed by checking all cuts of the graphs, which is expensive in computation. Computing the values of all these metrics is a time-consuming operation for large graphs.

Chapter 3

$\mathcal{R}$-energy for Evaluating Robustness of Dynamic Networks

In this chapter, we define the $\mathcal{R}$-energy (Gao *et al.*, 2013) as a new measure of network robustness based on the spectral analysis of the normalized Laplacian matrix. Compared to the existing robustness metrics, such as the set of connectivity measurements and the set of expansion measurements, our proposed $\mathcal{R}$-energy mainly has two advantages. First, $\mathcal{R}$-energy can evaluate the robustness of disconnected networks. However, all existing robustness measurements cannot be applied for evaluating the robustness of disconnected networks. Second, it is efficient to be computed with a time complexity of $O(|V| + |E|)$, where V and E are the vertex set and edge set of the network, respectively. As shown in the empirical study, our proposed algorithm takes as little as 40 seconds to compute $\mathcal{R}$-energy for a network with about 5M vertices and 69M edges. We also apply our proposed $\mathcal{R}$-energy to detect events occurring in a dynamic Twitter network with about 130K users and discover interesting weekly tweeting trends.

3.1 Introduction

The popularity of web, mobile phones, and other portable devices has propelled the growth of large-scale social networks such as Facebook and Twitter. These networks dynamically evolve as users join and leave and as their interaction intensity changes over time. To characterize the strength of these large-scale networks, we need some measurements for their robustness.

The ability to measure the robustness of networks can benefit several useful applications. For example, in a phone call network, dense and frequent calls among users in the network reduce the likelihood of churn. The similar observation can be found from online social networks. Network robustness is also studied in other applications such as disease transmission (Ball *et al.*, 1997; Eubank *et al.*, 2004), network security (Hasegawa and Masuda, 2011), etc. For example, the robustness of IP networks affects service quality and security. Service providers therefore aim to monitor, manage, and optimize their networks to keep their networks robust.

As today's networks are usually of very large scale, efficient measurement of network robustness is a challenge task. There are several previously proposed robustness measures mentioned in Chapter 2. They include node connectivity and edge connectivity proposed by Dekker and Colbert (2004), algebraic connectivity proposed by Jamakovic and Van Mieghem (2008), and Fiedler (1973), edge expansion (Hoory *et al.*, 2006), and vertex expansion (Bobkov *et al.*, 2000). However, these measures have the following shortcomings:

- They are only applicable to connected networks. Even though a highly robust giant component exists in a network with very few connected components, the network is considered not robust at all as all these measures return zero values.
- They quantify network robustness via using a specific (optimal) combinations of nodes (for node connectivity), a specific combination of edges (for edge connectivity), and a specific eigenvalue (for algebraic connectivity). For example, the network in Figure 2.8(b) is intuitively more robust than another network in Figure 2.8(a). However, the node, edge, algebraic connectivity and vertex expansion in Table 2.2 show that the robustness of the two networks are the same.
- They are difficult to scale for large networks of millions vertices and edges. Even though the edge expansion measure correctly tells us that the network in Figure 2.8(b) is more robust than the one in Figure 2.8(a), it is computed by checking all cuts of the network, an expensive operation. For algebraic connectivity, we need to compute the second smallest eigenvalue of the Laplacian matrix. For node

connectivity, edge connectivity, and vertex expansion, we have to check all cuts of the network. These are all time-consuming operations for the large networks.

In this chapter, we aim to address the problem of efficiently measuring network robustness, which should be defined in a principled way. As the same network may contain one or more connected components over time, our network robustness should be able to cope with the dynamicity of network evolution. We summarize our contribution to the study of network robustness as follows:

- We propose R-energy as an efficient measure for network non-robustness. Network robustness is thus the inverse of R-energy. The new measure, defined based on normalized Laplacian matrix, demonstrates several nice properties. It can also handle networks with multiple connected components and can be computed with good time complexity $O(|V| + |E|)$, where V and E are node set and edge set of a network.
- We apply R-energy to both synthetic and real networks. For a network with close to 5M vertices and 69M edges, the computation takes not more than 40 seconds. This shows that R-energy can cope with large scale networks comfortably.
- We further apply R-energy to a dynamic Twitter community with about 130K users to detect events and regular trend patterns that affect the network robustness. We empirically show that several significant events can be detected, and that users tend to be more active engaging each other on Sundays and Mondays, but not on Saturdays.

3.2 Related Work

3.2.1 *Robustness*

The traditional network robustness measures, node connectivity, and edge connectivity were proposed by Dekker and Colbert (2004). Graph expansion can also be used to measure network robustness. Different formulations of expander give rise to different measures of expander, e.g., edge expansion (Hoory *et al.*, 2006), vertex expansion (Bobkov *et al.*, 2000), and spectral expansion (Malliaros *et al.*, 2012). Larger edge or vertex expansions indicate less bottleneck inside a network. Nevertheless, these measures do not work well for networks with multiple connected components.

Jamakovic and Mieghem proposed to use the second smallest eigenvalue of the Laplacian matrix, also known as algebraic connectivity, to measure network robustness (Jamakovic and Van Mieghem, 2008; Fiedler, 1973). Malliaros *et al.* (2012) described the relationship between algebraic connectivity and node/edge connectivities. According to Cheeger's Inequality, Chung found that the expansion of a graph is closely related to the spectral gap between the largest and the second largest eigenvalues of adjacency matrix. Malliaros *et al.* confirmed the findings of Chung in Malliaros *et al.* (2012). This measure is however costly to compute and is sensitive to the network size. Hence, it is not appropriate for comparing networks of different sizes. Albert *et al.* (2000) used diameter to measure robustness of networks, but the measure does not capture network connectivity, which should be considered in robustness measures.

3.2.2 *Graph Energy*

The energy of a graph G has always been defined to be some form of deviation of eigenvalues of some graph matrix from the mean of eigenvalues. For example, Gutman defined graph energy on an adjacency matrix as the absolute deviation of eigenvalues from the mean of eigenvalues which is zero for any adjacency matrix (Gutman, 1978). In Robbiano and Jimenez (2009) and Zhou (2010), *Laplacian energy* has been defined on the *combinatorial Laplacian matrix*. In Cavers *et al.* (2010), *normalized Laplacian energy* is defined on the *normalized Laplacian matrix* in a similar manner.

Day and So (2007, 2008) studied graph energy changes with edge or vertex removals. There are some existing works which derive the lower and upper bounds for different energy definitions including Gutman's graph energy (Balakrishnan, 2004), Laplacian energy (Robbiano and Jimenez, 2009; Zhou, 2010; Zhou *et al.*, 2008) and normalized Laplacian energy (Cavers *et al.*, 2010). They are not appropriate measures for network robustness of a graph as computing them would be time costly.

3.3 R-energy

In Chapter 2, we have introduced the normalized Laplacian matrix and random walk to model graphs. In this section, we will discuss the connection between transition probabilities and normalized Laplacian matrix. After that, we will define $\mathcal{R}$-energy.

We denote

$$0 = \zeta_1 \leq \zeta_2 \leq \cdots \leq \zeta_n \tag{3.1}$$

as the eigenvalues of normalized Laplacian matrix N_G. There are several important properties about the eigenvalues of the normalized Laplacian matrix as presented in Lemma 3.1.

Lemma 3.1. *The eigenvalues of the normalized Laplacian matrix of a graph with n vertices satisfy the following properties:*

(1) $0 \leq \zeta_2 \leq \frac{n}{n-1} \leq \zeta_n \leq 2$;
(2) $\zeta_2 = \cdots = \zeta_n = \frac{n}{n-1}$ *if and only if G is a clique*;
(3) $\zeta_n = 2$ *if and only if G is a biclique*;
(4) *G has at least i connected components if and only if $\zeta_j = 0$, for $j = 1, 2, \ldots, i$.*

Property (1) says that all eigenvalues of the normalized Laplacian matrix range from 0 to 2. As a special case, when all except the smallest eigenvalue equal $\frac{n}{n-1}$, the graph is a clique as shown in Property (2). Property (3) states that the largest eigenvalue takes the upper bound value 2, the graph will be a biclique. A network therefore resemble a biclique when the largest eigenvalue is close to 2, or a clique when many eigenvalues are close to $\frac{n}{n-1}$. Property (4) states that each additional connected component corresponds to having the next smaller eigenvalue assigned with a zero value. ζ_1 is therefore 0 in any network.

3.3.1 *2-step Commute Probability*

Consider a graph $G = (V, E)$ with an adjacency matrix A_G and a degree matrix D_G, the transition probability matrix can be defined as

$$P = D_G^{-1} \cdot A_G.$$

Furthermore, the rule of random walk can be expressed by the simple equation:

$$W^t = P \cdot W^{t-1} = p^2 \cdot W^{t-2} = \cdots = P^t \cdot W^0, \qquad (3.2)$$

where W^0 represents the initial state of the random walk and W^t represents the state after t steps.

Nevertheless P is not a symmetric matrix, and this complicates its eigenvalue analysis. An important fact is that the eigenvalues of normalized Laplacian matrix N_G are closely related to the eigenvalues of P. With this, we can use the $N(G)$ to analyze spectrum for random walker.

Lemma 3.2. *Let* $\zeta_1, \ldots, \zeta_n$ *be the eigenvalues of* $N(G)$. *P have the eigenvalues equal to* $1 - \zeta_i$, *for* $i = 1, 2, \ldots, n$.

Proof. Note that

$$N_G = I - D_G^{-1/2} A_G D_G^{-1/2} = D_G^{1/2}(I - P)D_G^{-1/2}.$$

Suppose that v is an eigenvector of N_G, with eigenvalue ζ. We have

$$N_G \cdot v = \zeta \cdot v.$$

Let $q = D_G^{-1/2} \cdot v$, then,

$$\zeta \cdot v = D_G^{1/2}(I - P)D_G^{-1/2} \cdot v = D_G^{1/2}(I - P) \cdot q. \qquad (3.3)$$

By multiplying by $D_G^{-1/2}$ to Equation (3.3), we obtain

$$(I - P) \cdot q = \zeta \cdot D_G^{-1/2} \cdot v = \zeta \cdot q.$$

Therefore, q is an eigenvector of $I - P$ with eigenvalue ζ.   □

Based on the spectral analysis of the normalized Laplacian matrix, our proposed robustness metric is closely related to **2-step commute probability** of vertices in the random walk.

Definition 3.1 (2-step Commute Probability). In terms of the random walk rule shown in Equation (3.2), each entry p_{ij}^t of P^t is the probability that, starting at v_i, the walker reaches v_j in exactly t steps. Specially, the entry p_{ii}^2 represents the probability of reaching v_i from v_i in exactly two steps. This is also known as the **2-step commute probability** of vertex v_i. Computationally,

$$p_{ii}^2 = \sum_{j=1}^{n} p_{ij} \cdot p_{ji}.$$

The 2-step commute probability is very important as it measures the possibility of a random walk returning to vertex v_i after two steps. A lower value suggests that the walker starting from v_i is less likely to return in two steps, but more likely to visit the other vertices. That is, the vertex has high degree, and is well connected.

Example 3.1. Figures 2.8(a) and 2.8(b) show two undirected graphs with five vertices in a circle. Thus, the transition probability matrixes can be derived as

$$P = \begin{pmatrix} 0 & \frac{1}{2} & \frac{1}{2} & 0 & 0 \\ \frac{1}{2} & 0 & 0 & \frac{1}{2} & 0 \\ \frac{1}{2} & 0 & 0 & 0 & \frac{1}{2} \\ 0 & \frac{1}{2} & 0 & 0 & \frac{1}{2} \\ 0 & 0 & \frac{1}{2} & \frac{1}{2} & 0 \end{pmatrix}, \quad Q = \begin{pmatrix} 0 & \frac{1}{3} & \frac{1}{3} & \frac{1}{3} & 0 \\ \frac{1}{2} & 0 & 0 & \frac{1}{2} & 0 \\ \frac{1}{2} & 0 & 0 & 0 & \frac{1}{2} \\ \frac{1}{3} & \frac{1}{3} & 0 & 0 & \frac{1}{3} \\ 0 & 0 & \frac{1}{2} & \frac{1}{2} & 0 \end{pmatrix}.$$

We then compute the 2-step commute probabilities of vertex v_3 as

$$p_{33}^2 = \sum_{j=1}^{5} p_{3j} \cdot p_{j3} = \frac{1}{2} \cdot \frac{1}{2} + 0 \cdot 0 + 0 \cdot 0 + 0 \cdot 0 + \frac{1}{2} \cdot \frac{1}{2} = \frac{1}{2},$$

$$q_{33}^2 = \sum_{j=1}^{5} p_{3j} \cdot p_{j3} = \frac{1}{2} \cdot \frac{1}{3} + 0 \cdot 0 + 0 \cdot 0 + 0 \cdot 0 + \frac{1}{2} \cdot \frac{1}{2} = \frac{5}{12}.$$

Comparing the two 2-step commute probabilities, we know that v_3 in Figure 2.8(b) can reach the other vertices more easily than that in Figure 2.8(a) which follows our intuition.

3.3.2 $\mathcal{R}$-energy

According to Lemma 3.1, for a network G that is sparsely connected and is far from being a clique, its ζ_2 is small but ζ_n is large. In contrast, a network that is densely connected and similar to a clique will have ζ_2 not much smaller than ζ_n. In other words, a robust network should have a small gap between ζ_2 and ζ_n. This gap between ζ_2 and ζ_n can therefore be used to measure network robustness.

In statistics, the range of a set of data values is measured by variability, which is defined by the gap between the largest and the smallest data values (Woodbury, 2002). For networks, we may use some variability measures over their eigenvalue sequence $\zeta_2, \zeta_3, \ldots, \zeta_n$. Recall that ζ_1 is always zero. Examples of such variability measures include variance, standard deviation, and relative variability (Woodbury, 2002). In the following definition, we use the variance of the eigenvalues to measure network robustness and call the new measure **robustness energy**.

Definition 3.2 (Robustness Energy). Let G be a network. The **robustness energy** (shorted in $\mathcal{R}$-energy) of G is defined as

$$\mathbb{E}_{\mathcal{R}}(G) := \frac{1}{n-1} \sum_{i=2}^{n} (\zeta_i - \overline{\zeta})^2,$$

where $\overline{\zeta} = \frac{1}{n-1} \sum_{i=2}^{n} \zeta_i$.

In the definition of $\mathcal{R}$-energy, we ignore the value of ζ_1 since its value is always 0, and only the gap between ζ_2 and ζ_n are important. Obviously, $\mathcal{R}$-energy is always non-negative, and the smaller $\mathcal{R}$-energy is, the more robust network is. This is because smaller variability of $\zeta_2, \zeta_3, \ldots, \zeta_n$ implies that the network is closer to a clique.

$\mathcal{R}$-energy can be used to measure the robustness of both connected and disconnected networks. Networks with multiple connected components will see larger variability of their eigenvalues (as more ζ_i's are zeros) leading to larger $\mathcal{R}$-energy values.

The naive approach to compute $\mathcal{R}$-energy after obtaining all eigenvalues of the normalized Laplacian matrix is computationally expensive. In the next subsection, we therefore analyze the spectrum of the normalized

Laplacian matrix and propose a simple and efficient approach to compute R-energy in $O(|V| + |E|)$ time complexity.

3.4 Computation of R-energy

3.4.1 Properties

To compute the variance of eigenvalues $\zeta_2, \zeta_3, \ldots, \zeta_n$, we compute the mean using Theorem 3.1.

Theorem 3.1. *The mean of eigenvalues $\zeta_2, \zeta_3, \ldots, \zeta_n$ of a network with n vertices, denoted as $\bar{\zeta}$, is $\frac{n}{n-1}$.*

Proof. According to linear algebra, the trace of a matrix is defined by the sum of all its diagonal elements, and this is also equal to the sum of all eigenvalues of the matrix. Recall Definition 2.13, each entry $N_G(i, j)$ of N_G (i.e., normalized Laplacian matrix) is as follows:

$$N_G(i, j) = \begin{cases} 1, & \text{if } i = j \text{ and } d(v_i) \neq 0; \\ -\dfrac{1}{\sqrt{d(v_i)d(v_j)}}, & \text{if } A_G(i, j) \neq 0; \\ 0, & \text{otherwise.} \end{cases} \tag{3.4}$$

Each diagonal element of N_G is therefore 1. Note that $\zeta_1 = 0$. Thus,

$$\frac{1}{n-1} \sum_{i=2}^{n} \zeta_i = \frac{1}{n-1} \sum_{i=1}^{n} \zeta_i = \frac{1}{n-1} \cdot \text{tr}(N_G) = \frac{n}{n-1},$$

where $\text{tr}(N_G)$ denotes the trace of matrix N_G.   □

With the mean of the eigenvalue sequence, we can now compute R-energy using Theorem 3.2.

Theorem 3.2. *The R-energy of G satisfies Equation (3.5).*

$$\mathbb{E}_{\mathcal{R}}(G) = \frac{1}{n-1} \sum_{i=1}^{n} \sum_{j \neq i}^{n} \frac{A_G(i, j)}{d(v_i)d(v_j)} - \frac{n}{(n-1)^2}. \tag{3.5}$$

Proof. According to Theorem 3.1, the $\mathcal{R}$-energy of G can be expressed as

$$\mathbb{E}_{\mathcal{R}}(G) = \frac{1}{n-1} \sum_{i=2}^{n} \left(\zeta_i - \frac{n}{n-1} \right)^2$$

$$= \frac{1}{n-1} \sum_{i=2}^{n} \zeta_i^2 - \frac{2n}{(n-1)^2} \sum_{i=2}^{n} \zeta_i + \frac{n^2}{(n-1)^2}$$

$$= \frac{1}{n-1} \sum_{i=1}^{n} \zeta_i^2 - \frac{n^2}{(n-1)^2}.$$

According to Equation (3.4), the ith diagonal element of $N(G)^2$ is

$$\sum_{j=1}^{n} N_G(i,j) N_G(j,i) = \sum_{j \neq i}^{n} \frac{A_G(i,j)}{d(v_i)d(v_j)} + 1.$$

Applying an important property of the trace, i.e., $\sum_{i=1}^{n} \zeta_i^2 = \mathrm{tr}(N(G)^2)$, we obtain the following:

$$\mathbb{E}_{\mathcal{R}}(G) = \frac{1}{n-1} \sum_{i=1}^{n} \sum_{j \neq i}^{n} \frac{A_G(i,j)}{d(v_i)d(v_j)} - \frac{n}{(n-1)^2}. \qquad \square$$

Interestingly, the first term of the above $\mathbb{E}_{\mathcal{R}}(G)$ equation represents the average 2-step commute probability of vertices in G. Recall that the 2-step commute probability of all vertices can be computed as

$$\frac{1}{n} \sum_{i=1}^{n} p_{ii}^2 = \frac{1}{n} \sum_{i=1}^{n} \sum_{j \neq i}^{n} p_{ij} \cdot p_{ji} = \frac{1}{n} \sum_{i=1}^{n} \sum_{j \neq i}^{n} \frac{A_G(i,j)}{d(v_i)d(v_j)}.$$

Equation (3.5) can be further simplified to Equations (3.6) and (3.7).

$$\mathbb{E}_{\mathcal{R}}(G) = \frac{n}{n-1} \left(\frac{1}{n} \sum_{i=1}^{n} \sum_{j \neq i}^{n} \frac{A_G(i,j)}{d(v_i)d(v_j)} - \frac{1}{n-1} \right), \qquad (3.6)$$

$$= \frac{1}{n-1} \sum_{(v_i,v_j) \in E} \frac{1}{d(v_i)d(v_j)} - \frac{n}{(n-1)^2}. \qquad (3.7)$$

The factor $\frac{n}{n-1}$ in Equation (3.6) can be considered as a reward factor for the network of n vertices. Larger graphs are therefore more robust due to monotonically decreasing $\frac{n}{n-1}$ as n increases. This factor facilitates the comparison of R-energy for networks with different sizes.

Note that the 2-step commute probability of a clique with n vertices is $\frac{1}{n-1}$. The right-hand side of Equation (3.6) is thus the difference between the average 2-step commute probability and the 2-step community probability of a clique with the same size. Hence, the R-energy of G combines the reward of network size with the difference between the 2-step commute probability of G and that of a clique.

3.4.2 *Computation*

As R-energy can be expressed by Equation (3.7), we can efficiently compute it by scanning all edges of the network after computing the degrees of vertices in the network. Algorithm 1 depicts the steps to compute the R-energy of a network. The algorithm consists of two main steps. One is to compute the degree of vertices (Lines 1–3). Another is to aggregate the 2-step commute probabilities of vertices at Lines 4–6. The R-energy is finally obtained at Line 7. Both the time and space complexities of the algorithm are $O(|V| + |E|)$.

Algorithm 1: *calEnergy(G)*

Input: input graph: $G = (V, E)$;
Output: the R-energy of G: e;
1 **for** *each vertex $v \in V$* **do**
2 $\quad$ $deg(v) = |\{u|(v, u) \in E\}|$;
3 **end**
4 **for** *each edge $(v, u) \in E$* **do**
5 $\quad$ $e \leftarrow e + \frac{1}{deg(v)deg(u)}$;
6 **end**
7 $e \leftarrow \frac{e}{n-1} - \frac{n}{(n-1)^2}$;
8 **return** e

Example 3.2. Using Algorithm 1, we can compute the $\mathcal{R}$-energies of networks shown in Figures 2.8(a) and 2.8(b). From the network in Figure 2.8(a),we can see the degree of vertices as follows:

$$d(v_1) = 2, d(v_2) = 2, d(v_3) = 2, d(v_4) = 2, d(v_5) = 2.$$

The values of $d(v_i)d(v_j)(v_i, v_j \in E)$ in Table 3.1.

Bringing the values into Equation (3.7), we can get the $\mathcal{R}$-energy of network in Figure 2.8(a) is 0.3125. Similarly, the $\mathcal{R}$-energy of network in Figure 2.8(b) is 0.2014. The $\mathcal{R}$-energy values of the networks match our intuition that the latter is more robust than the former.

Compared to other measures shown in Table 3.2, our proposed $\mathcal{R}$-energy measure is better than all existing robustness measures.

Similar to the existing normalized Laplacian energy (Cavers *et al.*, 2010), we can also define a robustness measure using absolute deviation of eigenvalue sequence $\zeta_2, \zeta_3, \ldots, \zeta_n$. The measure however cannot be computed efficiently.

$\mathcal{R}$-energy can measure the robustness of both connected and disconnected graphs. Suppose that network G has N connected components, denoted as $\{C_k\}_{k=1}^N$. In Equation (3.8), the energy is derived

Table 3.1: Partial results of $\mathcal{R}$-energy for in Figure 2.8(a).

Edge	$\deg(v_i) \deg(v_j)$
$(v_1, v_2), (v_2, v_1)$	4
$(v_1, v_3), (v_3, v_1)$	4
$(v_2, v_4), (v_4, v_2)$	4
$(v_4, v_5), (v_5, v_4)$	4
$(v_5, v_3), (v_3, v_5)$	4

Table 3.2: Robustness metrics for networks in Figure 2.8.

Graph	Connectivity			Expansion			$\mathcal{R}$-energy
	Node	Edge	Algebraic	Vertex	Edge	Cheeger	
Figure 2.8(a)	2	2	1.382	1	1	0.5	0.3125
Figure 2.8(b)	2	2	1.382	1	1	0.5	0.2014

by weighted sum of the average 2-step commute probability of vertices from each connected component.

$$\mathbb{E}_{\mathcal{R}}(G) = \frac{n}{n-1}\left(\sum_{k=1}^{N}\frac{n_k}{n}P_{C_k} - \frac{1}{n-1}\right), \tag{3.8}$$

where P_{C_k} is the average 2-step commute probability of vertices from connected component C_k in Equation (3.9).

$$P_{C_k} = \frac{1}{n_k}\sum_{(v_i,v_j)\in C_k}\frac{A_G(i,j)}{d(v_i)d(v_j)}, \quad k = 1,\ldots,N. \tag{3.9}$$

$\mathcal{R}$-energy therefore considers a large disconnected network G to be robust if G contains a robust giant component.

3.5 Robustness of Large Static Networks

In this section, we evaluate our proposed $\mathcal{R}$-energy and other robustness measures on static networks including synthetically created networks and some real-world networks. We design a set of experiments to compare the effectiveness and scalability of $\mathcal{R}$-energy with algebraic connectivity. We also seek to find any common patterns that appear in the networks. The experiments on synthetic networks were implemented in Matlab, while those on real networks were implemented in Java. They were all conducted on a dual core 64-bit processor with 3.06 GHz CPUs and 128 GB of RAM.

3.5.1 *Experimental Network*

Synthetic networks. We generate different synthetic networks of N ($1\,\text{K} \leq N \leq 30\,\text{K}$) vertices with power law degree distribution using the graph generation algorithm proposed by Palmer and Steffan (2000). Each synthetic network with N vertices is denoted by Syn_N. In essence, the algorithm starts with a graph with N vertices but no edges. It then assigns a degree k to each vertex v such that $\Pr[\deg(v) = k] \approx k^{-\alpha}$ where α is the exponent > 2. Finally, the vertices are processed in decreasing degree order, and are assigned neighbors according to their degrees.

Table 3.3: Descriptive statistics of real networks.

ID	Network	Vertices	Edges	Density
EP	Epinion	75,879	508,837	1.767×10^{-4}
WG	Web graph	875,713	5,105,039	1.331×10^{-5}
IT	Internet topology	1,696,415	11,095,298	7.710×10^{-6}
LJ	LiveJournal	4,846,609	68,475,391	5.830×10^{-6}

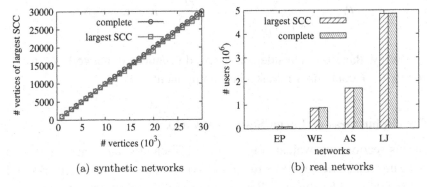

(a) synthetic networks   (b) real networks

Fig. 3.1: Size of largest SCCs (giant components).

Real networks. We use four static real networks with different sizes from Stanford Large Network Dataset Collection,[1] namely Epinions (Cho *et al.*, 2011), Web graph (Leskovec *et al.*, 2009), Internet topology (Leskovec *et al.*, 2005), and LiveJournal (Leskovec *et al.*, 2009). The descriptive statistics of these networks are shown in Table 3.3. In this work, we consider these networks unweighted and undirected.

To evaluate the algebraic connectivity, we extract the largest connected component and use it as a representative of the entire graph as there is always a giant component in each of these networks (Cohen *et al.*, 2000). Figures 3.1(a) and 3.1(b) confirm the giant components in both synthetic and real networks.

---

[1] http://snap.stanford.edu/data/index.html

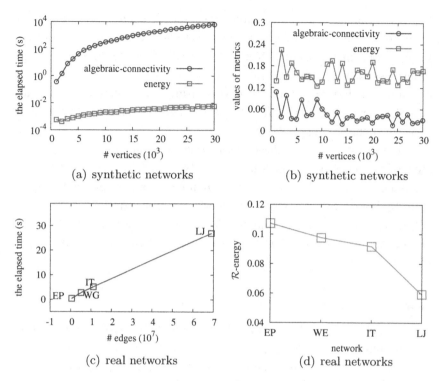

Fig. 3.2: Performance of computing the *R*-energy.

3.5.2 Efficiency and Scalability of R-energy

Figure 3.2(a) illustrates the *elapsed time* of computing both *R*-energy and algebraic connectivity on synthetic networks. We observe that Matlab takes almost one hour to compute the algebraic connectivity of the network with 30,000 vertices.[2] On the other hand, the elapsed time of *R*-energy computation for the same network is more than 4 order of magnitude faster than that of the algebraic connectivity for a large network. We further observe that the elapsed time for *R*-energy scales linearly with the number of edges making it ideal for networks with millions vertices.

---

[2]We employ Matlab function eigs($L, 2, -1.0$) to compute two eigenvalues which are closest to -1, i.e., the smallest and the second smallest eigenvalues of L, where L is a sparse matrix.

We evaluate the correlation between $\mathcal{R}$-energy and algebraic connectivity on the different synthetic networks to see if they produce similar robustness results. Note that small $\mathcal{R}$-energy suggests high robustness, while high algebraic connectivity suggests high robustness. As shown in Figure 3.2(b), the two measures are negatively correlated with Pearson correlation coefficient -0.62. This shows that the correlation between them is strong (<-0.5).

Figure 3.2(c) depicts the elapsed time of computing $\mathcal{R}$-energy and algebraic connectivity for four real networks. The elapsed time for algebraic connectivity for the smallest real network, i.e., Epinion, is more than 12 hours. For the largest network, LiveJournal (Leskovec *et al.*, 2009) with 4.8M vertices and 68.5M edges, $\mathcal{R}$-energy takes less than 40 seconds to compute. Figure 3.2(d) shows $\mathcal{R}$-energies for these real networks.

3.5.3 *Impact of Vertex Removal to $\mathcal{R}$-energy*

Complex networks with a heavy tail are known to be highly robust against random removal of vertices (Cohen *et al.*, 2000), but are hyper-sensitive to removal of high-degree vertices (Albert *et al.*, 2000; Callaway *et al.*, 2000). We would like to verify this using $\mathcal{R}$-energy measure.

We experiment with three vertex removal options, namely (a) remove in decreasing degree order, (b) remove in increasing degree order; and (c) remove in random order. For each option, after removing x fraction of vertices from the largest connected component, we compute $\mathcal{R}$-energy to measure the new network robustness. Figure 3.3 illustrates the $\mathcal{R}$-energy of resultant network for the three options compared with the $\mathcal{R}$-energy of the original network. From the figure, we obtain three important observations as follows.

Observation 3.1. Networks become less robust sooner when vertices of the highest degrees are removed.

Compared with the original graph, $\mathcal{R}$-energy increases sooner when vertices of the highest degrees are removed than when vertices of random degrees or small degrees are removed. This is the case since vertices of high degrees tend to have smaller 2-step commute probabilities.

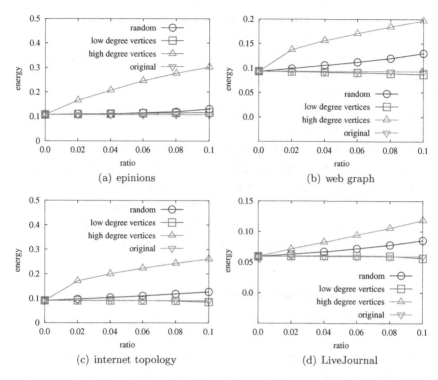

Fig. 3.3: *R*-energies of static graphs.

Removing them leads to an increase in average probability. Therefore, the network becomes less robust.

Observation 3.2. Networks remain robust or become slightly more robust when vertices of the smallest degrees are removed.

Figure 3.3 shows that *R*-energy remains constant or decreases slightly when vertices of the smallest degrees are removed from the network. Again, the smallest degree vertices have larger 2-step commute probabilities. Removing the smallest degree vertices results in little decrease in the average of the probabilities.

Observation 3.3. Networks become less robust when vertices are randomly removed. However, the change is slower than that of removing vertices of highest degrees.

This observation can be attributed to the fact that each vertex has a certain chance to decrease its degree when we remove vertices at random. That means the 2-step commute probability of each vertex increases with certain probability. However, vertices of smallest degree are more likely to be removed in scale-free networks. Hence, vertices of large 2-step commute probabilities are more likely to be removed leading to a decrease in graph energy.

The above three observations are also consistent to the results of Albert *et al.*'s (2000) work which uses diameter to measure robustness of networks. They found that scale-free networks are robust to random vertex removals, but not to removals of most connected vertices. The diameter of a network decreases when vertices of the smallest degrees are removed and the network becomes highly robust.

3.6 Detecting Events and Trends Using Robustness

Networks evolve with time, and so do their robustness. In this section, we apply $\mathcal{R}$-energy on dynamic and time-evolving Twitter network so as to evaluate robustness as a possible measure to detect events and trends. Before that, we use the number of replies or retweets to detect events. A few events are found due to intense fluctuation in these time series. Unlike the previous event and trend detection research which considers time series of messages or news articles generated in social media, our approach utilizes dynamic changes to network structure. These are the changes that cause a network to become suddenly more robust or less robust than usual.

3.6.1 *Data Collection*

Twitter is a popular microblogging site with users generating and sharing short message contents in real time (Java *et al.*, 2007). In this experiment, we first selected a set of Twitter users U who are the followers and followees of a small set of seed user accounts that belong to US politicians and analysts. These are the users who are more likely to tweet about political topics. We trawled the Twitter data generated by U from 1 May 2012 to 29 July 2012.

From U, we further selected users who write, reply, or retweet at least one tweet per month over three months. There are 129,056 such users, and we keep them in the user set U discarding the remaining users and their tweets. Each day, a subset of users in U may reply or retweet one another. We therefore construct a *reply network* and another *retweet network* for day t and denote them by $G^{RE}(t)$ and $G^{RT}(t)$, respectively. An undirected edge (u, v) is included in the reply network for day t if user u replies at least a tweet from user v, or user v replies at least a tweet from user u in day t. The edges in retweet network on day t are created in a similar manner.

3.6.2 Event Detection

We show the R-energies of $G^{RE}(t)$ and $G^{RT}(t)$ in Figures 3.4(a) and 3.4(b). To facilitate reading, we add vertical lines representing Sundays to the figures. From the figures, we aim to determine events that are characterized by bursts and drops of communication (replies or

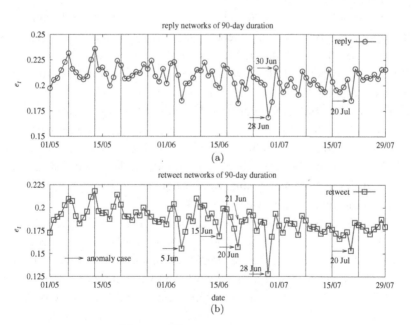

Fig. 3.4: R-energy on G^{RE} and G^{RT}.
Note: Vertical lines denote Sundays.

retweets) by many users. We call these the *internal* and *external events* as the former can be explained by the bursty content but not the latter. For example, a sport event may draw user attention away from tweeting about politics. In addition to event detection, we also want to explain internal events by searching the web.

Suppose $(e_1, e_2, \ldots, e_{90})$ is the sequence of $\mathcal{R}$-energy values. We calculate the absolute first-order difference of energy sequence, denoted as $(d_1, d_2, \ldots, d_{90})$, where $d_1 = 0$ and $d_{t+1} = |e_{t+1} - e_t|$ for $1 \leq t \leq 89$. Based on the mean and standard deviation of $\{d_t\}$, we can detect an event at time t' statistically if $|d_{t'} - \text{mean}(\{d_t\})| > \gamma \cdot \text{std.dev}(\{d_t\})$, where $\text{mean}(\{d_t\})$ and $\text{std.dev}(\{d_t\})$ denote the mean and standard deviation of $\{d_t\}$, respectively. In other words, an event is found when the absolute first-order difference deviates from mean more than γ times the standard deviation. However, mean is known to be sensitive to anomalies. We therefore employ trimmed mean, which is defined as the mean after discarding the smallest and largest $\tau\% \cdot d_t$ values. In this work, we set $\gamma = 3$ and $\tau = 5$ empirically.

To describe an event at day t, we need to extract relevant event description keywords from tweets (which can be replies or retweets) generated on the same day t. We denote the words extracted from reply tweets (or retweets) on day t by $W^{\text{RE}}(t)$ (or $W^{\text{RT}}(t)$) and the frequency of word $w \in W^{\text{RE}}(t)$ (or $W^{\text{RT}}(t)$) by $f^{\text{RE}}(w, t)$ (or $f^{\text{RT}}(w, t)$). We define the first-order frequency difference of word w for day t as $df^*(w, t) = f^*(w, t) - f^*(w, t - 1)$.[3] From $\{df^*(w, t)\}$, we derive the mean and standard deviation as $\text{mean}^*(w)$ and $\text{std.dev}^*(w)$, respectively.

Table 3.4 shows the means and standard deviations of absolute energy difference sequence and word frequency difference sequence of the dynamic reply and retweet networks.

Take the largest difference of energy from both G^{RE} and G^{RT} on 28 June 2012 as an example. The top three words from retweets with highest frequency difference are "tax","Obamacar" and "scotu" (**Supreme Court of United States**) after stopword removal and word stemming. By searching the web using these keywords, we verified that the Obamacare

---

[3]* denote RE or RT.

Table 3.4: Descriptive statistics of reply and retweet networks.

Network	Absolute energy diff.		Word frequency diff.	
	Mean($\{d_t\}$)	Std.dev($\{d_t\}$)	Mean*(w)	Std.dev*(w)
G^{RE}	0.0093	0.0075	23.5	145.8
G^{RT}	0.0098	0.0093	148.3	1230.2

healthcare law was upheld by the Supreme Court of United States, and there were concerns about tax increase as its outcome. This event attracted a lot of replies and retweets on June 28. The word frequency difference of "Obamacar" in retweets subsided quickly on 29 June 2012 as shown by a negative df^{RT} (*Obamacar*, 29 Jun) value.

For each day t, we define the *average frequency difference* of the three words w_1, w_2, and w_3 with highest $df^*(\cdot, t)$ as $M^*(t) = \frac{1}{3} \sum_{i=1}^{3} df^*(w_i, t)$. If $M^*(t)$ deviates far away from the mean mean*(w) w.r.t. the value std.dev*(w), an event is considered to happen on day t.

Formally, we define the normalized $M^*(t)$ on day t as

$$N^*(t) = \frac{M^*(t) - \text{mean}^*(w)}{\text{std.dev}^*(w)}.$$

The larger the $N^*(t)$ is, the more likely the top words are able to explain some event on t. Empirically, we use the words with $N^*(t) \geq 8$ to help us to explain internal events. On the other hand, an external event may prevent people from communicating in Twitter. In this case, $N^*(t)$ may be small due to very few users generating tweets. We nevertheless tried to use the frequent words on day t to search the web to confirm if an event is external.

Figure 3.5 illustrates the $N^*(t)$ values of both G^{RE} and G^{RT}. Table 3.5 lists seven events found from G^{RE} and G^{RT} using R-energy. The first column shows the date of event and $N^*(t)$ value. The second column shows the top three words derived by top frequency differences in G^{RE} or G^{RT} depending on which of the two networks is used to detect the event. The final column shows the description of events manually derived from the Google search results of the top words.

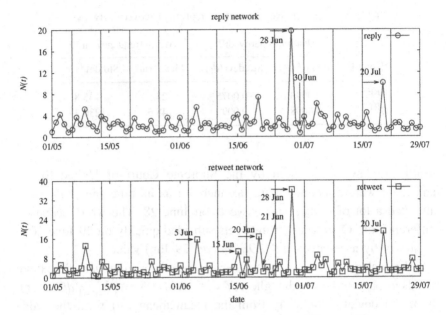

Fig. 3.5: Normalized difference of word frequencies on G^{RE} and G^{RT}.
Note: Vertical lines denote Sundays.

Instead of using $\mathcal{R}$-energy, we also experimented with time series of daily reply and retweet counts using a similar event detection method. Unlike the $\mathcal{R}$-energy time series, we could detect only two events on 28 June and 30 June, listed in Table 3.5. This is due to the fact that reply and retweet counts fluctuate a lot over time. We therefore detect fewer bursty events than that using $\mathcal{R}$-energy. The results also show that $\mathcal{R}$-energy can help detecting events that are different.

3.6.3 *Periodic Trend Pattern Detection*

Other than ad hoc events, Mann–Kendall trend test (Mann, 1945) indicates that a periodic pattern significantly exists in G^{RE} and G^{RT} of Figure 3.4. We also want to detect weekly trend patterns from the figure by examining the regularities in network energy changes. This weekly pattern can be even more distinct when the ad hoc events are removed.

In this section, we therefore focus on detecting weekly pattern. Based on a predefined threshold θ ($= 0.1 \times \text{mean}(\{d_t\})$), we first derive three kinds of energy changes from the previous day, namely (i) *energy*

Table 3.5: Detected events from G^{RE} and G^{RT}.

Date $(N^*(t), G^*)$	Event	Description
5 June (15.6, G^{RT})	wisconsin(21089) walker(20726) wirecal(16213)	Tom Barr. Wisconsin voters rejected a year-long effort to recall Gov. Scott Walker.
15 June (10.6, G^{RT})	obama(17652) immigr(11284) illeg(10588)	President Obama is way out of line with his June 15th immigration amnesty.
20 June (16.7, G^{RT})	fastandfuri(23295) holder(19991) obama(18974)	White House has asserted executive privilege on "fast and Furious" documents.
21 June (2.3, G^{RT})	lebron(3816) nba(2694) twitter(2517)	Twitter goes down in worst crash in 8 months.
28 June (36.2, G^{RT})	tax(52444) obamacar(51390) scotu(30247)	Obamacare is the largest tax increase in the history of the world.
30 June (1.7, G^{RE})	natgat(1898) republic(1061) storm(1049)	Honorable Bio visited California to bring the power loss.
20 July (10.0, G^{RT})	shoot(25860) gun(24103) aurora(20480)	A gunman killed 12 people at a midnight showing of the new Batman movie in Aurora, Colorado.

increase ("+"), (ii) *energy decrease* ("−"), and (iii) *insignificant change* (*null*). Given a day of a week x, e.g., Tuesday, we count the number of "+"s, "−"s, and *null*'s and denote them by $p(x)$, $n(x)$, and $null(x)$, respectively. After ignoring the ad hoc events, we increment $p(x)$ if the energy change is more than θ; increment $n(x)$ if the energy change is smaller than $-\theta$; or increment $null(x)$ otherwise. The proportions of "+"s and "−"s on x across multiple weeks can be defined as:

$$prop("+", x) = \frac{p(x)}{p(x) + n(x) + null(x)},$$

$$prop("-", x) = \frac{n(x)}{p(x) + n(x) + null(x)},$$

$$prop(null, x) = \frac{null(x)}{p(x) + n(x) + null(x)}.$$

Let $\max_{prop}(x)$ be maximum value of $prop("+", x)$, $prop("-", x)$ and $prop(null, x)$. We assign a label l to day x as follows:

$$l = \begin{cases} "+", & \text{if } prop("+", x) \text{ equal to } \max_{prop}(x); \\ "-", & \text{if } prop("-", x) \text{ equal to } \max_{prop}(x); \\ null, & \text{otherwise.} \end{cases} \qquad (3.10)$$

In case of $prop("+", x) = prop("-", x) = \max_{prop}(x)$, we assign a *null* label to the day x.

For example, suppose out of 13 weeks, there are 12 Mondays with "$-$"s, one with "$+$" and zero with *null*. The compositions of positive, negative, and null energy changes on Monday are 7.7%, 92.3%, and 0%, respectively. Monday therefore is assigned to "$-$". By assembling the proportions of positive, negative, null energy changes for different days of week, we obtain the *weekly trend pattern* of G^{RE} and G^{RT}.

Figure 3.6 illustrates the composition of weekly pattern for G^{RE} and G^{RT}. According to label assignment rule, we obtain the weekly trend pattern "$- - - + - + -$" for G^{RE}, and another weekly trend pattern "$- - - + + + -$" for G^{RT}. Other than Friday, the two weekly trend patterns obtained from G^{RE} and G^{RT} are very similar.

From the weekly trend pattern, we can casually conclude that users are less likely to tweet on Saturdays, but tweet a lot on Sundays as well as Mondays.

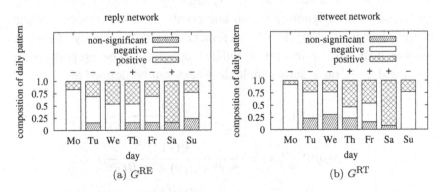

Fig. 3.6: Weekly pattern detecting.

3.7 Conclusion

Measuring and explaining the robustness of large-scale networks is an important and challenging task both in network science theories and applications. The robustness of a network is related to the connectivity of its vertices. In this chapter, based on the normalized Laplacian matrix, we define a new robustness measure called R-energy, which is closely related to the average 2-step commute probability. The computation of R-energy is highly efficient as it involves a single scan of the vertices and edges of the network. This new measure can therefore be applied to large dynamic networks. This paper also presents the results of applying R-energy to large dynamic Twitter networks so as to detect events and trends. Our empirical study shows that interesting events and trends can be found among tweeting users.

Chapter 4

Network Linkage Across Heterogeneous Networks

In this chapter, we propose an unsupervised method, collective network linkage (CNL) (Gao *et al.*, 2015), to link users across heterogeneous social networks. CNL incorporates heterogeneous attributes and social features unique to social network users, handles missing data, and performs in a collective manner. CNL is highly accurate and efficient even without training data. We evaluate CNL on reidentifying users for the same social network, as well as linking users across different social networks. Our experimental results on a Twitter network and another Foursquare network demonstrate that CNL performs very well for the above two tasks, and its accuracy is superior than the supervised Mobius approach.

4.1 Introduction

Today's information-based dynamic platforms are a convenient way for users to use numerous accounts of different online social networks simultaneously, such as Twitter, Facebook, and Foursquare, to enjoy diverse services. An urgent requirement is therefore to identify different accounts from different social networks that belong to the unique user. We call this the *network linkage problem*. There are several benefits accrued from a more complete set of user information through network linkage, and these include: (a) improved product recommendations which can be given to users whose preferences can be determined from a more complete user profile; (b) better insights into a user's complete social network when the latter is derived from the user's social networks at different sites (for example, one may realize that a user maintains her business relationships in one network and friendships in another); and (c) deeper understanding of how content diffuses from one network to

49

another, which may suggest the ability for the former to generate more original and interesting content. However, the task is non-trivial.

4.1.1 *Challenges*

Network linkage is a novel research problem. Other than lacking complete ground truth for evaluation, network linkage is also challenging due to the following reasons:

Heterogeneity: User attributes and behaviors can differ vastly across social networks due to the different site designs. For instance, Foursquare displays the initial of the last name of users (e.g., "Michael S."), while Twitter displays full last name (e.g., "Michael Smith"). Foursquare maintains gender attribute, but Twitter does not.

Missing and incomplete data: The same users may not provide the same attribute information when they are in different social networks. This could be attributed to input errors or users' intentional omission.

Large scale: The possible pairs of users from different social networks to be matched is enormous. Suppose two social networks have M and N user accounts, respectively, there will be $M \times N$ user pairs to be considered, making network linkage a high complexity task.

User connectivity: Users in social networks are connected to one another. Linking any pair of users thus has to consider the neighbors of these two users in addition to their attributes.

4.1.2 *Objectives and Contributions*

We formulate network linkage as an unsupervised learning problem. We manifest that network linkage can be performed with promising accuracy even without training data, which are usually arduous and costly to obtain in large scale. As will be described in the following subsection, there is thus far no unsupervised network linkage method that addresses the outlined challenges.

Our proposed approach is called the collective network linkage (CNL). Compared with the well-known probabilistic record linkage method (Fellegi and Sunter, 1969; Sadinle and Fienberg, 2013), CNL is also an unsupervised approach and addresses the four challenges highlighted earlier. It utilizes the exponential family to model hetero-geneous user behavior, handles missing data in the unsupervised framework, employs locality sensitive hashing (LSH) to scale-up to the large-scale networks, and evaluates the social similarity in a collective manner. In summary, our main contributions are as follows.

- We introduce a unified approach to model user attributes, which include their personal attributes, behaviors, and social connections, and to derive their similarity functions. The similarity values are modeled probabilistically so as to form the building blocks of our proposed method.
- We develop an unsupervised learning method called CNL that incorporates heterogeneous attributes and social features unique to social network users, handles missing data, and performs in an iterative manner to update social features.
- To handle large-scale network linkage, we incorporate LSH into CNL. With LSH, CNL runs very efficiently while maintaining high accuracy in the linkage results. In addition, it can handle cold start in computing similarities for social features and attributes with missing data.
- We evaluate our algorithm against baselines on two real Twitter and Foursquare datasets. Experimental results illustrate that CNL outperforms baselines in linking users across different social networks. We further evaluate CNL against supervised method, and the result is also promising.

4.2 Related Work

4.2.1 *Network Linkage Across Social Platforms*

There are some existing works which attempt to address the problem of network linkage across different social platforms. They are however based on supervised approach, while this section focuses on the unsupervised approach.

Linking users across different social networks was first formulated by Zafarani and Liu (2009). They proposed a simple approach to link users by their usernames. As mentioned in Liu *et al.* (2013), this approach however may not always work well for different social networking sites. Liu *et al.* (2013) considered username popularity and proposed a heuristic rule to automatically determine if two accounts from different sites with the same username belong to the same person. The rule labeled user account pairs are then used for training a classifier for network linkage. Zafarani and Liu (2013) proposed more than 400 features from language, writing styles, and similarity of usernames. All these features make use of username attribute only. Zhang *et al.* (2014) proposed a probabilistic classifier to solve the online social network profile linkage. Kong *et al.* (2013) considered network linkage as a link prediction problem across heterogeneous social networks. They focused on social features, spatial distribution features, temporal features and content features, leaving out username. Iofciu *et al.* (2011) developed a method to link users in social tagging systems combining the edit distance of usernames and the similarity between the set of tags adopted by the users. SiGMa is an iterative and greedy algorithm for linking two knowledge bases (Lacoste-Julien *et al.*, 2013). However, our approach is different from SiGMa since SiGMa can only link two knowledge graphs and our approach can link two sets of social network users with or without social structures.

In addition, some literatures on the view of privacy protection consider the network linkage across different social networks. When a user from a social platform is given, (Goga *et al.*, 2013) tried to find the identical users from another social networks. The problem is very different from our task. Lu *et al.*'s (2014) and Shen and Jin's (2014) approaches are also the supervised, and cannot handle the network linkage without any ground-truth pairs. Narayanan and Shmatikov's (2009) study reidentifies the annonymized users from different social network via purely exploiting the network topology.

Unfortunately, these above-mentioned methods do not provide a common framework for comparing attributes of users in network linkage, nor do they offer solution to address attribute and behavior heterogeneity as well as missing data issues. Finally, they do not explore the social connectivity among users to improve network linkage accuracy. Liu *et al.* (2014) proposed a supervised approach to handle missing data, which simply replaces missing values with zeros. Such an approach is non-ideal as it distorts the distribution of attribute values.

4.2.2 Record Linkage

Linking user across different social networks is related to the traditional record linkage problem (Ravikumar and Cohen, 2004; Koudas *et al.*, 2006; Yakout *et al.*, 2010), sometimes also known as data matching (Scannapieco *et al.*, 2007), duplicate detection (Bilenko and Mooney, 2003; Christen, 2012; Elmagarmid *et al.*, 2007), data cleaning (Chaudhuri *et al.*, 2003), data disambiguation (Cucerzan, 2007), and entity resolution (Whang *et al.*, 2009) etc. Solutions of record linkage problem can be grouped into two types: deterministic linkage approach (Roos and Wajda, 1991; Grannis *et al.*, 2002) and probabilistic linkage approach (Fellegi and Sunter, 1969; DuVall *et al.*, 2010). Deterministic linkage approach is usually rule-based, involving exact one-to-one matching of username and other user attributes (Roos and Wajda, 1991; Grannis *et al.*, 2002). It works well only the linkage problem is simple or when there is special domain knowledge about matching users. Probabilistic linkage methods (Fellegi and Sunter, 1969; Sadinle and Fienberg, 2013), on the other hand, involve the derivation for a given user pair the linkage probability estimated from all observed agreements and disagreements of user attribute values. Fellegi and Sunter provided the formal mathematical foundations of probabilistic record linkage (Fellegi and Sunter, 1969). They introduced a variety of principled ways to estimate matching probabilities directly from the records being matched. However, existing Fellegi–Sunter-based approaches consider two attributes to be similar if they are identical or their similarity value is up to a predefined threshold. For two strings "Michael S." and "Michael Smith", they may be treated as dissimilar attributes. Our paper represents the first attempt that extends this probability record linkage to link users across social networks. Our proposed approach incorporates various similarities of heterogeneous attributes, dynamically captures the social similarity, and handles missing data.

4.3 Problem Definition

Let A and B be two social networks. For simplicity, we use A and B to denote the two sets of users from the two social networks. Let α and β represent the observed user attributes from A and B, respectively. That is, $\alpha(A) = \{\alpha(a)|a \in A\}$ and $\beta(B) = \{\beta(b)|b \in B\}$, where $\alpha(a)$

and $\beta(b)$ represent the attribute feature vectors of individuals a and b. Given the set of all user pairs

$$R = \alpha(A) \times \beta(B) = \{(\alpha(a), \beta(b)) | a \in A, b \in B\}.$$

Definition 4.1. The **network linkage problem** is to determine the matched pairs M and unmatched pairs U in R, i.e.,

$$M = \{(\alpha(a), \beta(b)) | a = b, a \in A, b \in B\},$$

$$U = \{(\alpha(a), \beta(b)) | a \neq b, a \in A, b \in B\},$$

where $a = b$ means that a and b belong to the same user, while $a \neq b$ means that a and b belong to different users.

When $(\alpha(a), \beta(b)) \in M$, we say that a is linked to b. Conversely, when $(\alpha(a), \beta(b)) \in U$, we say that a is not linked to b. Also, we may ideally want $R = M \cup U$, but in practice R is a very large set. One would therefore like to consider a smaller R that includes M using some filtering technique(s).

4.4 Solution Overview

In this section, we present the main framework of collective network linkage for matching different accounts on heterogeneous network which belong to the unique user. For better understanding of the algorithm, we display a simple running example to explain the framework.

4.4.1 *Framework*

CNL method consists of three building blocks corresponding to the three steps below.

Step 1: User attribute modeling and similarity function definitions. We determine a set of similarity functions γ_i's between attributes from α and β so as to use them for linking users. Each similarity function is designed for comparing user attributes and social connections. CNL models the similarity of user pairs to accommodate heterogeneous attributes using different probability distributions of their similarity values. More details about these similarity functions will be discussed in Section 4.5.1.

Step 2: Parameter learning. Given each similarity function γ_i, CNL models the similarity values of user pairs using two different probability distribution functions, one for matched user pairs and another for unmatched user pairs. The parameter learning step is used to infer parameters of the two distributions. More details will be provided in Section 4.5.2.

Step 3: User pair scoring and linkage outcome assignment. In this step, the matched scores of user pairs are used to judge if they belong to the matched or unmatched pair sets, i.e., M or U.

CNL considers both discrete and continuous similarities as a wider range of probability distributions from the exponential family to model the similarity values of matched and unmatched user pairs (in Step 1). The exponential family handles the first challenge via integrating the heterogenous attribute types into CNL, including string, numeric, set, distribution, etc., that exist in the network linkage task.

Other than heterogenous user attributes, CNL also links users based on their social similarities. In particular, a pair of users u_k and u_l are more likely to match each other when they share many common social connections. To compute social similarity between u_k and u_l, we however require the outcome of linkage for their friends. This suggests an iterative network linkage process which is also part of the CNL algorithm. In other words, Steps 1–3 will have to be repeated to revise the social similarity of user pairs based on the linkage results from the previous iteration.

We now present the full CNL algorithm in Algorithm 2. In this algorithm, PP maintains the set of matched user pairs. We assume there are $m - 1$ similarity functions $(s[1], \ldots, s[m - 1])$ for non-social attributes and the mth similarity function (i.e., $s[m]$) for social connectivity. Initially, as we do not have any matched user pairs, $s[m]$ is zero for all pairs. The remaining pairs will have their non-social attribute similarity values computed. With the similarity values, CNL performs parameter learning to determine Θ, the distributions of matched and unmatched pairs corresponding to each user attribute. Using the learned distributions, CNL computes the probabilities that a user pair r_j belongs to matched pairs M and U, respectively (i.e., $P(r_j \in M | \gamma^j, \widehat{\Theta})$, and $P(r_j \in U | \gamma^j, \widehat{\Theta})$).

Algorithm 2: Collective Network Linkage Algorithm

Input: Two user sets, A and B, with social structures, number of top result K;

Output: Matched user pairs (PP) and their match scores;

1   $R \leftarrow \emptyset$; $j \leftarrow 0$;

2   // Step 1: attribute modeling and similarity function definition **for** *each $a \in A$* **do**

3 | **for** *each $b \in B$* **do**

4 | | $r \leftarrow (\alpha(a), \alpha(b))$;

5 | | **for** $i = 1$ *to* $m - 1$ **do** $s[i] \leftarrow \gamma_i(r)$;

6 | | $s[m] \leftarrow 0$; //social similarity is set to 0

7 | | $R \leftarrow R \cup \{(r, s)\}$;

8 | **end**

9   **end**

10   // Step 2: Parameter learning **while** *parameter set Θ has not converged* **do**

11 | $eStep(R)$; //handle unknown and missing data

12 | $mStep(R)$; //maximize log-likelihood

13   **end**

14   // Step 3: User pair scoring and linkage outcome assignment **for** $r_j \in R$ **do** $sc_j \leftarrow \log \frac{P(r_j \in M | \gamma^j, \widehat{\Theta})}{P(r_j \in U | \gamma^j, \widehat{\Theta})}$;

15   $PP \leftarrow$ top-K pairs in R with the largest match scores;

16   // Repeat Steps 1 to 3 considering social similarity **repeat**

17 | **for** *each $r_j \in R$* **do**

18 | | $s^j[m] \leftarrow$ social similarity w.r.t. PP;

19 | **end**

20 | **while** *parameter set Θ has not converged* **do**

21 | | $eStep(R)$; //handle unknown and missing data

22 | | $mStep(R)$; //maximize log-likelihood

23 | **end**

24 | **for** $r_j \in R$ **do** $sc_j \leftarrow \log \frac{P(r_j \in M | \gamma^j, \widehat{\Theta})}{P(r_j \in U | \gamma^j, \widehat{\Theta})}$;

25 | $PP \leftarrow$ top-K pairs in R with the largest match scores;

26   **until** *Termination Condition is satisfied*;

27   **return** PP *and* $\{w\}$

In Step 3, a match score sc_j is computed and the highest scored pairs are assigned the matched pair labels, PP. The pairs can be selected based on some thresholds (i.e., top-K).

Once the matched user pairs are determined, CNL will revise the social similarity values of the remaining user pairs, learn a new set of parameters Θ, and compute the new match scores sc_j by repeating Steps 1–3. As long as the new matched user pairs are found or Θ changes significantly between iterations, we may repeat the process adding more matched user pairs to PP.

4.4.2 *Running Example*

For example, Figure 4.1 gives an example execution of a simple CNL for network linkage. We employ CNL to link two networks between

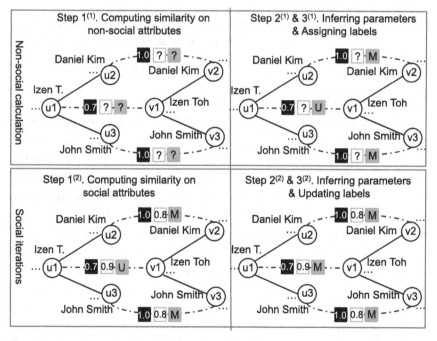

Fig. 4.1: Running example of CNL (A solid line represents the social connection. A dashed line represents a pair of users from different networks. Non-social and social similarities are shown in black and white boxes, respectively; labels are shown in grey boxes. A question mark indicates a missing value).

which we have three special pairs (u_i, v_i), $i = 1, 2, 3$. In the initial state (Step $1^{(1)}$ at Lines 2–9 of Algorithm 2), only non-social similarities are computed. Thus, no social similarity has yet been computed for the pair (u_i, v_i). In Steps $2^{(1)}$ and $3^{(1)}$ (Lines 10–15 of Algorithm 2), parameters are inferred and labels are predicted. Due to the low similarity of name, (u_1, v_1) is predicted as an unmatched pair, the other two are the matched pairs. Then, we repeatedly run Steps $1^{(2)}$, $2^{(2)}$ and $3^{(2)}$ considering social connections. In Step $1^{(2)}$ (Lines 17–19 of Algorithm 2), social similarities are computed. In Steps $2^{(2)}$ and $3^{(2)}$ (Lines 20–25 of Algorithm 2), parameters are inferred and labels are updated. Due to the high similarity on social connections, (u_1, v_1) is updated as a matched pair. Then, the algorithm repeats Steps $1^{(2)}$–$3^{(2)}$ until the termination condition is satisfied.

4.5 Linkage Algorithm

In this section, we will detail the technique employed in three steps, namely similarity computation for different attributes of various types, parameter learning in EM algorithm, and how we predict matched pairs.

4.5.1 *User Attribute and Social Similarity*

A user may have multiple attributes in different social networks. Some of them are personal demographic attributes, e.g., username, gender, age, and origin. These can be of different data types (e.g., numeric, text, string, categorical, etc.). Some may be attributes modeling user behaviors. Examples are URLs visited, bag of words used, and login patterns. These attributes can be represented in set and distribution types. A user may also have different social connectivities in different social networks. These can be friends, followers, or followees.

We derive M and U based on how similar a pair of users are in every user attribute and social connectivity. Suppose, we have m similarity functions that can be defined over the user attributes and social connectivity. These similarity functions can be represented as an m-dimensional vector γ. For each user profile pair $r_j = \big(\alpha(a), \beta(b)\big) \in R$, $\gamma^j = \gamma(r_j) = (\gamma_1(r_j), \gamma_2(r_j), \ldots, \gamma_m(r_j))$, where $\gamma_i^j = \gamma_i(r_j)$ is the ith similarity value for users a and b.

In Koudas *et al.* (2006), they proposed some similarity functions for common attribute types. However, these are not enough for network linkage task. In the following, we examine a few attribute types and their respective similarity functions. These attribute types are not meant to be exhaustive but are sufficient for most cases. The similarities can be modeled using some distribution(s), each with a different set of parameters.

Numerical: Categorical attributes are very common. Examples are the city, country, gender, and language used by the user. The similarity between two categorical values is 1 if they are identical, and 0 otherwise. We can model the probability distribution of the similarity values of a category attribute using a Bernoulli distribution.

String: Examples of numerical attribute are age, salary, weight, and height. The similarity between two numerical values can be computed as the difference between two values. The similarity value can be modeled as a discrete or continuous distribution. These include Poisson, Gaussian, and Exponential distributions.

String is a common attribute type. Examples are username, affiliation, etc. The similarity between two strings can be computed by *Edit distance, longest common subsequence, longest common substring,* Jaccard Coefficient (Zafarani and Liu, 2013), etc. Some string similarity requires each string value to be represented as a bag of n-grams. A naive string similarity function can be defined by the Jaccard Coefficient (JC) of n-grams representing the two strings.

The above string similarity functions can be further adapted for specific types of string attributes. For example, person name is a special type of string which carries some special semantics. Person name usually consists of first, middle, and last names, and the similarity between two person names has to be derived with some knowledge about the name structure. Considering username as an example, we provide an improved JC to evaluate the similarity between two names strings.

Without loss of generality, assume that two user names $u_i = \langle w_{i1} \ w_{i2} \ w_{i3} \rangle, i = 1, 2$ (assuming that each name consists of first, middle, and last names). The similarity between these two names can be computed by weighted word-level JC as

$$\text{sim}(u_1, u_2) = \frac{1}{3} \sum_{i=1}^{3} p(w_{1i}, w_{2i}) JC(w_{1i}, w_{2i}),$$

where $p(w_{1i}, w_{2i})$ is the joint observed probability of w_{1i} and w_{2i}. It is computed by $p(w_{1i}) \times p(w_{2i})$ simply.

In statistical language modeling, the probability of observing a word w, denoted in characters as $w = c_1 c_2 \cdots c_k$, can be approximated by an n-gram model as

$$p(w) = \prod_{i=1}^{k} p(c_i | c_{i-(n-1)} \cdots c_{i-1}).$$

For example, to estimate the probability of word *Alif*, the probability using a bi-gram model can be estimated by

$$p(Alif) \approx p(A|\text{`` ''})p(l|A)p(i|l)p(f|i)P(\text{`` ''}|f),$$

where $p(A|\text{`` ''})$ and $P(\text{`` ''}|f)$ denote the probabilities of characters A and f being the head and tail of the word, respectively.

Suppose two social networks do not share the same name format. For example, one can find u_1, "Michael Smith", from Twitter and u_2, "Michael S.", from Foursquare. u_2 is represented as $\langle w_{21}\ c_{22} \rangle$, where c_{22} is the first character of the last name. In this case, the last item of the weighted word-level Jaccard Coefficient can be modified as $I_{c_{22} \sim w_{12}} p(w_{12}, \text{``}c_{22}\text{.''})$, where $I_{c_{22} \sim w_{12}}$ is an indicator function which returns 1 if c_{22} matches the first character of w_{12}, and 0 otherwise.

Set. Set attribute can be used to represent user behavior. For example, user written text can be represented by a set of words, and user visitation information can be represented by a set of locations. The similarity between two sets can be defined by Jaccard Coefficient, Dice Index, and Cosine Coefficient. We can use Gaussian or exponential function to model the similarity values of user pairs with these attribute types.

Distribution. Distribution is also a multi-valued attribute that is ideal for representing a user's behavior, e.g., distribution of used words and distribution of visited locations. Distribution value can also be learned from topic models, such as LDA and PLSA (Blei *et al.*, 2003). The similarity between two distributions with the same dimension can be defined by Jensen–Shannon divergence, Squared Euclidean, inner product, etc.

Social connections. The social connections of a user are essentially a set of other related users. The standard social similarity measures, such as SimRank (Zheng *et al.*, 2013), Jaccard Coefficient, and Adamic/Adar Coefficient (Liben-Nowell and Kleinberg, 2007), are defined for a single social network. Here, we extend the definitions of Jaccard Coefficient and Adamic/Adar Coefficient for network linkage since it is difficult to iteratively compute SimRank for it.

Extended Adamic/Adar. Let a and b be the two users from different social networks, and $\Gamma(a)$ and $\Gamma(b)$ be the social friends of a and b, respectively. Let the common matched friends $\Gamma(a) \cap \Gamma(b)$ be $CF(a, b)$. We extend the Adamic/Adar measure for two heterogeneous networks as

$$AA(a, b) = \sum_{\forall (a_i, b_j) \in CF(a,b)} \log^{-1} \left(\frac{|\Gamma(a_i)| + |\Gamma(b_j)|}{2} + 1 \right).$$

The Adamic/Adar measure are weighted for the common friends by their average degrees of two social networks with a smoothing. $AA(a, b)$ is large (implying that a and b are likely the same user) when a and b have many common matched friends with few neighbors in both social networks. We also extend Jaccard Coefficient for social similarity as follows.

Extended Jaccard Coefficient. Let u be a user in a network, and S be a user set. We define the weighted degree of u on $\Gamma(u)\backslash S$ as

$$\text{Deg}(u, S) = \sum_{u_i \in \Gamma(u)\backslash S} \log^{-1} (|\Gamma(u_i)| + 1).$$

With the extended Adamic/Adar Coefficient, we now define the extended Jaccard Coefficient across different networks (traditionally,

$\text{Jaccard}(A, B) = \frac{|A \cap B|}{|A \cap B| + |A \setminus B| + |B \setminus A|})$ as

$$\text{EJC}(a, b) = \frac{AA(a, b)}{AA(a, b) + \text{Deg}(a, \Gamma(b)) + \text{Deg}(b, \Gamma(a))}.$$

4.5.2 Parameter Learning and Matching Score Computation

Given a set of m similarity functions γ defined over user attributes and social connections, CNL learns the parameters of similarity value distributions for matched and unmatched user pairs based on exponential family distributions. With these learned similarity value distributions, CNL infers whether a user pair r_j is a matched or unmatched pair by estimating probabilities $P(r_j \in M | \gamma^j, \Theta)$ and $P(r_j \in U | \gamma^j, \Theta)$.

4.5.2.1 Likelihood

Assume that $P(r_j \in M | \Theta) = p$. Thus, $P(r_j \in U | \Theta) = 1 - p$. Notice that $P(r_j \in M | \gamma^j, \Theta) = 1 - P(r_j \in U | \gamma^j, \Theta)$.

Let l_j be 1 if $r_j \in M$, and 0 otherwise. We define $x_j = (l_j, \gamma^j)$ as the "complete data" vector for r_j. Applying Bayes' rule, the probability of observation x_j under parameters Θ can be defined as

$$P(x_j | \Theta) = \left[P(\gamma^j, r_j \in M | \Theta) \right]^{l_j} \left[P(\gamma^j, r_j \in U | \Theta) \right]^{(1-l_j)}$$
$$= \left[p \cdot P(\gamma^j | r_j \in M, \Theta) \right]^{l_j} \left[(1 - p) \cdot P(\gamma^j | r_j \in U, \Theta) \right]^{(1-l_j)}.$$

Let $l^j = (l_j, 1 - l_j)$, and thus we obtain the log-likelihood for sample $X = \{x_j : j = 1, 2, \dots, N\}$ as

$$\mathbb{L}(\Theta | X) = \sum_{j=1}^{N} l^j \left[\log P(\gamma^j | r_j \in M, \Theta), \log P(\gamma^j | r_j \in U, \Theta) \right]^T$$

$$+ \sum_{j=1}^{N} l^j \left[\log p, \log (1 - p) \right]^T.$$

4.5.2.2 Exponential Family

The exponential family is a convenient and widely used family of distributions. Distributions in the exponential family appeal to the machine learning community as some good properties of MLE which is a function of the sufficient statistic and the best unbiased estimator, etc. (Wainwright and Jordan, 2008).

An exponential family is a set of $\{f(x; \theta) : \theta \in \Theta \subset \mathbb{R}^k\}$ of PDFs or PMFs on $\mathbb{R}^d$ s.t. $f(x; \theta) = h(x) \exp(\theta^T S(x) - z(\theta))$, where θ is the natural parameter of a distribution, $S(x)$ is a sufficient statistic for θ. The exponential family contains as special cases most of the standard discrete and continuous distributions that we use for practical modeling, such as the Gaussian, Poisson, Binomial, multinomial, exponential, Gamma, multivariate Gaussian, etc. Gaussian, Exponential, and Poisson are distributions of infinity, while some similarity functions are of limited range. Fortunately, Gaussian, Exponential, and Poisson are long-tail distributions. We can use a truncated Gaussian, Exponential, or Poisson to model similarities. The difference between the original distributions and the truncated distributions is a normalized constant. We can therefore use the original distributions to estimate the truncated distributions.

To estimate $P(\gamma^j | r_j \in M, \Theta)$ and $P(\gamma^j | r_j \in U, \Theta)$, we assume that γ^j is drawn from a distribution of exponential family, and use the simplifying assumption that the components of vector γ^j are conditional independent with respect to the state of the indicator l_j, i.e.,

$$P(\gamma_i^j | r_j \in M, \Theta) \sim f_{1,i}(\gamma_i^j; \theta_{1,i}), \quad \text{for } i = 1, \ldots, m,$$

$$P(\gamma_i^j | r_j \in U, \Theta) \sim f_{2,i}(\gamma_i^j; \theta_{2,i}), \quad \text{for } i = 1, \ldots, m,$$

where $f_{.,i}(\cdot; \cdot)$ (shorted in $f_{.,i}$) is a PDF or PMF from the exponential family.

We obtain the log-likelihood as

$$\mathbb{L}(\Theta | X) \propto \sum_{j=1}^{N} l^j \left[\sum_{i=1}^{m} \theta_{1,i}^T S_{1,i}(\gamma_i^j), \sum_{i=1}^{m} \theta_{2,i}^T S_{2,i}(\gamma_i^j) \right]^T$$

$$- \sum_{j=1}^{N} l^j \left[\sum_{i=1}^{m} z_{1,i}(\theta_{1,i}), \sum_{i=1}^{m} z_{2,i}(\theta_{2,i}) \right]^T$$

$$+ \sum_{j=1}^{N} l^j \left[\log p, \log(1 - p) \right]^T. \tag{4.1}$$

4.5.2.3 *Maximum Likelihood Estimator*

Since the values of l^j are unknown, we estimate the parameters $\Theta = \{p, \theta_{1,i}, \theta_{2,i}, \text{ for } i = 1, \ldots, m\}$ via maximum likelihood estimation using the EM algorithm. The EM algorithm begins with estimates of the unknown parameters $\hat{\Theta}$ and consists of iterative applications of the E-step and M-step until the desired precision is obtained.

E-step. For the E-step, we find the expectations of l_j. Since the conditional distribution of l_j given γ^j and $\Theta^{(k-1)}$ is $l_j|\gamma^j, \Theta^{(k-1)} \sim \text{Bin}(1, p_j^{(k)})$ with

$$
\begin{aligned}
p_j^{(k)} &= P(l_j = 1|\gamma^j, \Theta^{(k-1)}) \\
&= \frac{P(r_j \in M, \gamma^j|\Theta^{(k-1)})}{P(\gamma^j|\Theta^{(k-1)})} \\
&= \frac{P(r_j \in M, \gamma^j|\Theta^{(k-1)})}{P(r_j \in M, \gamma^j|\Theta^{(k-1)}) + P(r_j \in U, \gamma^j|\Theta^{(k-1)})} \\
&= \frac{P(r_j \in M)P(\gamma^j|r_j \in M, \Theta^{(k-1)})}{P(r_j \in M)P(\gamma^j|r_j \in M, \Theta^{(k-1)})) + P(r_j \in U)P(\gamma^j|r_j \in U, \Theta^{(k-1)})} \\
&= \frac{p^{(k-1)} \cdot \Pi_{i=1}^{m} f_{1,i}}{p^{(k-1)} \cdot \Pi_{i=1}^{m} f_{1,i} + (1 - p^{(k-1)}) \cdot \Pi_{i=1}^{m} f_{2,i}}.
\end{aligned}
$$

By substituting $p_j^{(k)}$ for l_j, we obtain the expectation function.

M-step. For the M-step, when we estimate the values of $l_j^{(k)} = p_j^{(k)}$ in E-step, for $i = 1, \ldots, m$, we take derivatives of the log-likelihood as follows:

$$
\frac{\partial \mathbb{L}(\Theta|X)}{\partial p} = \sum_{j=1}^{N} \left(\frac{l_j^{(k)}}{p} - \frac{1 - l_j^{(k)}}{1 - p} \right), \tag{4.2}
$$

$$
\frac{\partial \mathbb{L}(\Theta|X)}{\partial \theta_{1,i}} = \sum_{j=1}^{N} l_j^{(k)} \left(S_{1,i}(\gamma_i^j) - \frac{\partial z_{1,i}(\theta_{1,i})}{\partial \theta_{1,i}} \right), \tag{4.3}
$$

$$
\frac{\partial \mathbb{L}(\Theta|X)}{\partial \theta_{2,i}} = \sum_{j=1}^{N} (1 - l_j^{(k)}) \left(S_{2,i}(\gamma_i^j) - \frac{\partial z_{2,i}(\theta_{2,i})}{\partial \theta_{2,i}} \right). \tag{4.4}
$$

Table 4.1: MLEs of parameters for matched groups.

Distribution	MLE for matched group
Multinomial	$p_{1,i}^{h,(k)} = \dfrac{\sum_{j=1}^{N} l_j^{(k)} I_{\gamma_i^j = h}}{\sum_{j=1}^{N} l_j^{(k)}}$
Gaussian	$\mu_{1,i}^{(k)} = \dfrac{\sum_{j=1}^{N} l_j^{(k)} \gamma^j}{\sum_{j=1}^{N} l_j^{(k)}}$
	$(\sigma_{1,i}^{(k)})^2 = \dfrac{\sum_{j=1}^{N} l_j^{(k)} (\gamma^j - \mu_{1,i}^{(k)})^2}{\sum_{j=1}^{N} l_j^{(k)}}$
Exponential	$\lambda_{1,i}^{(k)} = \dfrac{\sum_{j=1}^{N} l_j^{(k)}}{\sum_{j=1}^{N} l_j^{(k)} \gamma_i^j}$

Due to $\frac{\partial z_{.,i}(\theta_{.,i})}{\partial \theta_{.,i}} = E_{\theta_{.,i}}\left(S_{.,i}(\gamma_i)\right)$ ($\cdot$ can be 1 or 2), MLEs of parameters can be obtained.

While we specify the distributions of γ_i, $i = 1, \ldots, m$, we can estimate the parameters in the M-step of the k-iteration. The probability p can be estimated as $p^{(k)} = \frac{\sum_{j=1}^{N} l_j^{(k)}}{N}$. The MLEs of parameters for some distributions of the matched groups in the model are summarized in Table 4.1. In Equation (4.4), the MLEs of parameters for the unmatched groups are very similar to those of the matched groups. Note that parameter learning of CNL consists of E-step and M-step, and applies the normal EM algorithm. Thus, CNL converges to the MLE if the log-likelihood is unimodal (Wu, 1983).

4.5.2.4 *Missing Data*

In the presence of missing data, the sample X can be denoted as $(X_{\text{obs}}, X_{\text{mis}})$, where X_{obs} denotes the observed data and X_{mis} denotes the unobserved or "missing" data. More specifically, if $\Theta^{(0)}$ is the initial values for the parameters, during the k-iteration, the E-step of the EM algorithm computes

$$Q(\Theta; \Theta^{(k-1)}) = E\left(\mathbb{L}(\Theta|X)|X_{\text{obs}}, \Theta^{(k-1)}\right).$$

Due to missing data, values $S_{1,i}(\gamma_i^j)$ and $S_{2,i}(\gamma_i^j)$ in Equation (4.1) are missing. The value $Q(\Theta; \Theta^{(k-1)})$ can be computed by substituting $E(S_{1,i}(\gamma_i^j)|\Theta^{(k-1)})$ and $E(S_{2,i}(\gamma_i^j)|\Theta^{(k-1)})$ for $S_{1,i}(\gamma_i^j)$ and $S_{2,i}(\gamma_i^j)$ in Equations (4.3) and (4.4), respectively.

4.5.2.5 *Matching Score Computation*

Once parameters Θ are estimated, CNL determines whether user pair r_j belongs to matched pair or unmatched pair by computing its match score:

$$sc^j = \log\left(\frac{P(r_j \in M|\gamma^j, \hat{\Theta})}{P(r_j \in U|\gamma^j, \hat{\Theta})}\right) \propto \sum_{i=1}^{m} sc_i^j,$$

where

$$sc_i^j = \theta_{1,i}^T S_{1,i}(\gamma_i^j) - \theta_{2,i}^T S_{2,i}(\gamma_i^j) - z_{1,i}(\theta_{1,i}) + z_{2,i}(\theta_{2,i}).$$

$sc_i^j = 0$ when γ_i^j is missing. $P(r_j \in M|\gamma^j, \hat{\Theta}) > P(r_j \in U|\gamma^j, \hat{\Theta})$ if $sc^j > 0$, i.e., r_j is more likely a matched pair if sc^j is much larger than 0. The top K user pairs according to sc^j are then designated as matched pairs.

4.5.3 *Scale-up CNL*

From Lines 2–9 of Algorithm 2, the network linkage across different social platforms is computationally expensive. The major computational cost is significantly impacted by generating candidate pairs and computing social similarity.

Blocking methods (Christen, 2012), such as n-gram indexing and sorted neighborhood, are used in linkage systems to reduce the number of candidate comparison pairs to a feasible number while still maintaining accuracy. However, the number of candidate pair comparisons with two networks of n users containing in b blocks is $O(\frac{n^2}{b})$. The common problem is the large number of candidate comparison pairs if b is small. In this chapter, we therefore employ LSH to block users in terms of their names. The reason for employing LSH on usernames is due to the fact that humans tend to have similar behavior patterns when selecting usernames across different social networks (Zafarani and Liu, 2013). The advantage of LSH is its ease of scale-up to large networks since the number of blocks can be arbitrarily large.

4.5.3.1 *Reducing Candidate Pairs*

In terms of usernames, we build an LSH schema which hashes users into buckets, where each bucket corresponds to a block. The basic idea is to hash users so that users associated with similar usernames are mapped to the same buckets with high probability. LSH consists of three essential components:

Shingling: Based on universal set of bi-grams from usernames, a username can be converted into a binary vector.

Minhashing: Using minhashing technique, the vector can be mapped to a signature. Furthermore, two users with the same signature are mapped to the same bucket.

Locality-sensitive hashing: For each user, multiple signatures are generated. Two users across different social networks become a candidate pair if they are found in the same bucket.

There are two important parameters for an LSH schema: the length of a signature (t) and the number of signatures for each user (g). Let I be the universal set of bi-grams. The number of buckets can be $|I|^t$, which can be very large.

4.5.3.2 *Speeding up Social Similarity Computation*

Two users from different social networks are more likely to be the same person if they have more common matched friends. Due to the high complexity of computing social similarity, we can also use the LSH schema to speed up the computation of social similarity. Compared to the LSH schema on usernames, the only difference is the universal set. For LSH on social feature, the universal set is the collection of users who are in the ground-truth matched pairs or in the predicted pairs. LSH also consists of the above-mentioned three essential components. After building LSH on social feature, a pair of users is more likely to be found from the same bucket if they share many matched friends. We only compute the social similarity of a pair if two users are mapped into one of the buckets. Otherwise, we treat the social similarity as a missing value if two users are mapped into different buckets.

4.6 Experiments

In this section, our CNL algorithm is systematically evaluated with different experimental settings and compared with the baseline methods using real social networks. We conduct two experiments to compare CNL with the baseline methods using real social networks. In Experiment 1, we perform the network linkage task between two identical networks (also known as the *self-linkage* task) in which there is clearly a ground truth one-to-one matching between users from identical networks. To better understand the behavior of CNL, we introduce noise to the user attributes for self-linkage. In Experiment 2, we perform heterogeneous network linkage between two large real social networks Twitter and Foursquare.

4.6.1 *Dataset and Settings*

4.6.1.1 *Datasets*

We use two large-scale real social networks in our experiments.

A. Twitter: We gathered a set of 73,109 Twitter users, who indicate Singapore as their profile location, associated with 1,376,412 social relationships. The dataset consists of user profiles, two-way follow relationships, and tweets from 1 July to 30 November 2013.

B. Foursquare (4sq): From the above dataset, we extracted tweets generated by check-in's performed by 4sq users who are also Twitter users in our dataset. We then gathered the Singapore-based friends of these users and crawled the profiles of 206,039 users associated with 5,139,432 social relationships, as well as their check-in's and tips in 4sq.

Between the above two networks, there are 3,534 ground-truth matched user pairs as declared by the users in these two networks.

This ground-truth is only partial as many users do not reveal their user accounts on both Twitter and 4sq. We employ three shared user attributes from both the networks for network linkage, i.e., usernames, language, and temporal behavior. Temporal behavior is the temporal patterns for tweeting in Twitter and checking in 4sq. We model username, language, and temporal behavior as string, categorical, and distribution variables, and evaluate their similarity by improved Jaccard, binary value, and Jensen–Shannon divergence, respectively.

4.6.1.2 *Comparative Methods*

We evaluate CNL and the baseline methods considering: (a) all attributes vs. all but username and (b) the distribution functions for attribute similarity. Option (a) allows us to study the methods' performance when not using username, a very discriminative attribute. Option (b) studies the effect of not using the most appropriate distribution.

We evaluate our proposed method CNL in its different variants: CNL_{F-E}, CNL_{nonN-E} and CNL_{nonN-G}. The F option denotes all attributes are used, while, $nonN$ option denotes the use of all attributes except username. The $-E$ and $-G$ options denote the use of an Exponential distribution and a Gaussian one for modeling each continuous similarity value, respectively. For example, CNL_{nonN-E} is CNL using all attributes except username and Exponential distributions to model the temporal and social similarity values. We choose two baseline methods: the non-collective Network Linkage (NL) and Mobius. NL does not adopt social similarity and hence performs one iterative of matching user pairs (i.e., Lines 1–15 of Algorithm 2). Like CNL, the NL method has several variants, namely NL_{F-E}, NL_{nonN-E}, and NL_{nonN-G}. Since there is no existing unsupervised approach to link users across different social networks, we compare our CNL with Mobius which is a supervised learning method proposed by Zafarani and Liu (2013). The method relies on username attribute only to link users from two networks. Implementing Mobius in our data context, we can only extract 66 features instead of 400 features since many features used in Mobius are not applicable. We classify them into individual features (e.g., username length, alphabet distribution, entropy of username alphabet, and username observation likelihood) and user pair features (e.g., longest common substring, longest common subsequence, edit distance, Jaccard Coefficient, and Jensen–Shannon divergence). However, the set of 66 features contains the top five crucial features mentioned in Mobius.

4.6.1.3 *Evaluation Measures*

We evaluate the methods using Precision@K and Recall@K. Precision@K is the fraction of the user pairs in the top-K result that are correctly matched. Recall@K is the fraction of ground truth matched users that appear among the top-K results. To evaluate scalability, we measure the elapsed time and number of candidate pairs.

4.6.2 *User Self-linkage Evaluation*

We first evaluate the methods in the self-linkage task. The task is designed such that we know the complete ground truth matched user pairs. We then evaluate the methods against the complete ground truth. Using the **Twitter** network, we create a new network $TW_N(\delta)$ which is a sub-network of **Twitter** with some noises injected into the username. Let N denote the size of the sub-network, and δ denote the probability of each character in the username being changed to another random character.

We randomly selected eight well-connected users and their ego-networks. This gives as a sub-network $TW_{1109}(\delta)$. Figure 4.2 illustrates the distributions of feature similarity for matched and unmatched pairs. We can observe that the Jaccard Coefficient between usernames, Jensen–Shannon divergence between user temporal behaviors, and the extended Jaccard Coefficient between social structures follow positive skewed distributions, and the language matching follows a binomial or multinomial distribution. We then assign an appropriate distribution from the exponential family for each similarity.

Comparing with unsupervised baselines. The accuracy of the methods for self-linking $TW_{1109}(0\%)$ is shown in Table 4.2. Since username is noise free, we exclude it from the NL- and CNL-based methods. The results show that: (1) social similarity improves the performance for

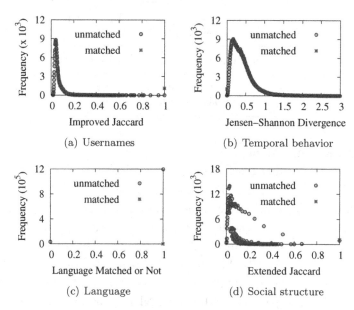

Fig. 4.2: Similarity distributions for self-linkage on $TW_{1109}(0\%)$.

Table 4.2: Performance on $TW_{1109}(0\%)$.

| K | NL_{nonN-E} | | NL_{nonN-G} | | CNL_{nonN-E} | | CNL_{nonN-G} | |
	Pre.	Rec.	Pre.	Rec.	Pre.	Rec.	Pre.	Rec.
200	0.985	0.178	0.398	0.072	**0.990***	0.179	0.511	0.092
400	0.978	0.353	0.393	0.142	**0.995***	0.359	0.504	0.182
600	0.983	0.532	0.387	0.209	**0.996***	0.539	0.497	0.269
800	0.981	0.708	0.383	0.276	**0.998***	0.720	0.489	0.353
1000	**0.977***	0.885	0.375	0.338	0.942	0.840	0.481	0.434
1109	**0.938***	0.938	0.372	0.372	0.898	0.888	0.474	0.474
1200	**0.889***	0.938	0.369	0.399	0.844	0.888	0.466	0.504

*The improvements are statistically significant for $p > 0.05$ judged by paired t-test.

smaller K and (2) the choice of distribution function severely affects the performance of the algorithm. For larger K, the error of social similarity becomes larger when more unmatched pairs are assigned as matching ones. In summary, social similarity is useful to link users across different social networks even when username is not given.

Table 4.3: Precision comparing CNL_{F-E} with Mobius for self-linking $TW_{1109}(10\%)$.

Approach	LibSVM	Logistic	Naive Bayes
Mobius	0.915	0.896	0.882
CNL_{F-E}	**0.946**	**0.937**	**0.911**

Comparing with Mobius. In Table 4.3, we compare CNL_{F-E} with Mobius. We construct new training and testing datasets which contain 1,109 ground truth pairs and randomly selected 1,109 non-ground truth pairs, respectively. We build three classifiers and use 10-fold cross-validation to evaluate the performance of Mobius. For each fold, we count the number of matched pairs predicted by Mobius, denoted as K_i $(i = 1, 2, \ldots, 10)$. Let K' be $\sum_{i=1}^{10} K_i$. In Table 4.3, Mobius row is the micro-average precision of the positive instances for different classifiers. To compare with Mobius, CNL_{F-E} assigns positive labels to the top-K' pairs among 2,218 pairs in the training and testing data of Mobius. We find that CNL_{F-E} outperforms Mobius. The possible reasons could be that: (1) CNL_{F-E} considers more meaningful features than Mobius; and (2) Mobius' performance is affected by the number of networks for training.

Varying δ. Figure 4.3 demonstrates the performance of CNL_{F-E} on $TW_{1109}(\delta)$ by varying δ from 0% to 20%. Figures 4.3(a)–4.3(c) illustrate that Precision@K, Recall@K, and F_1@K, are reduced by larger δ, i.e., more noise is added into usernames. When 20% noise is added into username, the precision and recall of the top-1109 result are around 60%.

Scalability of CNL. We perform self-linkage on larger networks to evaluate the scalability of the methods. The task involves linking between users in $TW_N(10\%)$. Figure 4.4 depicts the results by varying N of $TW_N(10\%)$ from 10,000 to 70,000. The required number of users are randomly selected from the full user set while keeping the network connected. The option L denotes that we use Locality Sensitive Hashing to block users for linking the large networks. For example, CNL_{LF-E} is CNL_{F-E} using LSH to block users. As shown in Figures 4.4(a)

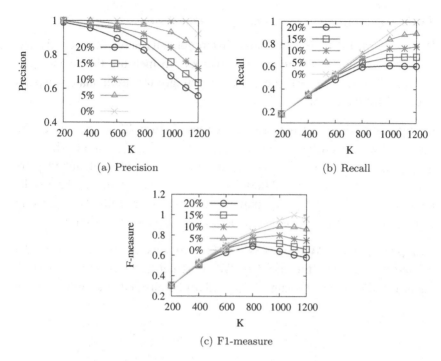

(a) Precision

(b) Recall

(c) F1-measure

Fig. 4.3: CNL_{F-E}'s performance vs. noise on $TW_{1109}(\delta)$.

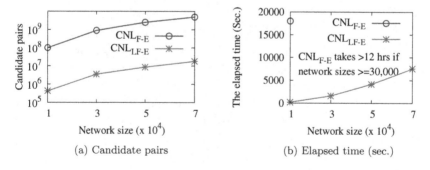

(a) Candidate pairs

(b) Elapsed time (sec.)

Fig. 4.4: Scalability of CNL on $TW_N(10\%)$.

and 4.4(b), CNL_{LF-E} only considers less than 1% of the candidate pairs after applying the blocking strategy, and requires only several hours to run. CNL_{F-E} (without blocking), on the other hand, takes more than 12 hours to run when the network size is no less than 30,000.

4.6.3 *Heterogeneous User Linkage Evaluation*

We now turn to linking two large heterogeneous networks, namely our complete Twitter and Foursquare networks. To measure the accuracy of network linkage, we use the 3,534 partial ground truth matched pairs declared by the users.

Comparing with unsupervised baselines. Figure 4.5 demonstrates the precision and recall for NL_{LF-E}, NL_{LF-G}, CNL_{LF-E}, and CNL_{LF-G}. We observe that more than 60% pairs in the ground-truth linked pairs can be found in the top-12,000 (i.e., K = 12,000) results. The results also indicate that CNL_{LF-E} outperforms the other methods, and using Exponential distribution is better than using Gaussian distribution.

Comparing with Mobius. CNL links two sets of N users from the ground truth of **Twitter** and **4sq**. We construct new training and testing datasets which focus the same N ground truth pairs and randomly selected

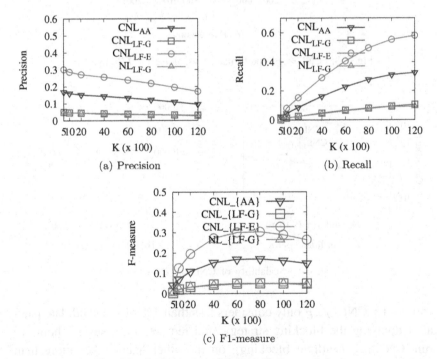

(a) Precision

(b) Recall

(c) F1-measure

Fig. 4.5: Performance of linking Twitter and 4sq.

Table 4.4: Precision comparing CNL_{F-E} with Mobius.

Network size	LibSVM		Logistic		Naive Bayes	
	Mobius	CNL	Mobius	CNL	Mobius	CNL
1,000	0.861	**0.895**	0.774	**0.832**	0.771	**0.825**
1,500	0.840	**0.903**	0.774	**0.859**	0.803	**0.861**
2,000	0.861	**0.915**	0.767	**0.851**	0.769	**0.822**
2,500	0.856	**0.902**	0.799	**0.861**	0.791	**0.845**
3,000	0.851	**0.888**	0.810	**0.873**	0.791	**0.855**
3,500	0.830	**0.871**	0.807	**0.879**	0.811	**0.867**

N non-ground truth pairs, respectively. The setup of the experiment is similar to the self-linkage task. In Table 4.4, Mobius row is the micro-average precision of the positive instances for different classifiers. To compare with Mobius, CNL_{F-E} assigns the positive labels to the top-K' pairs among $2N$ pairs in the training and testing data of Mobius. We find that CNL_{F-E} outperforms Mobius. The possible reasons for this have been mentioned earlier.

Varying parameters in LSH setting. Figure 4.6 shows the precision of CNL_{LF-E} by varying parameters in LSH setting. Figures 4.6(a)–4.6(d) illustrate that the performance of CNL_{LF-E} is stable as we change the parameters g and t for LSH building, where g and t denote the number of groups and the length of a signature in a LSH. We can conclude that: (1) CNL_{LF-E} obtains a promising trade-off between scalability and effectiveness; (2) username and social connection are two paramount features for network linkage since performance is not affected when CNL only considers the pairs with high similarities in username and social connection as candidates.

Performance for different iterations. Figure 4.7 manifests the performance of different iterations of CNL_{LF-E}. On the one hand, we can find that the 1st-5th iterations improve the performance of CNL_{LF-E} significantly. Note that 0th-iteration is the algorithm NL_{LF-E} without any social iterations. The result therefore illustrates that social connection is beneficial to improve the performance of CNL. On the

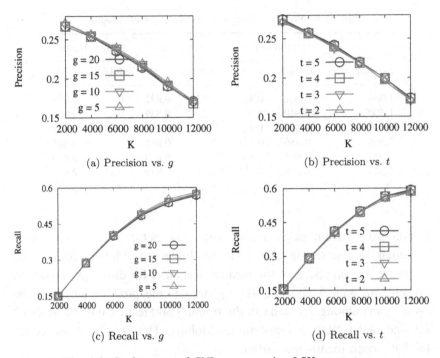

(a) Precision vs. g (b) Precision vs. t

(c) Recall vs. g (d) Recall vs. t

Fig. 4.6: Performance of CNL_{LF-E} varying LSH parameters.

other hand, CNL is overwhelmingly efficient, and converges after six iterations.

Manually judged top results of CNL_{LF-E}. We now examine the top matched user pairs returned by CNL_{LF-E} which are not among the known partial ground truth user pairs. We invited five volunteers to manually annotate the top-300 matched pairs of CNL_{LF-E} with our developed visualization tool.[1] Two user accounts are judged to be a matched pair when (a) their profile pages contain evidence of the same user (e.g., same profile picture), and (b) there are other external evidence (e.g., the user maintains Instagram profile mentioning her Twitter and Foursquare accounts). When the user pair consists of clearly different users, it is annotated as an unmatched pair. The remaining user pairs are assigned the undetermined label.

---

[1] www.research.larc.smu.edu.sg/linky

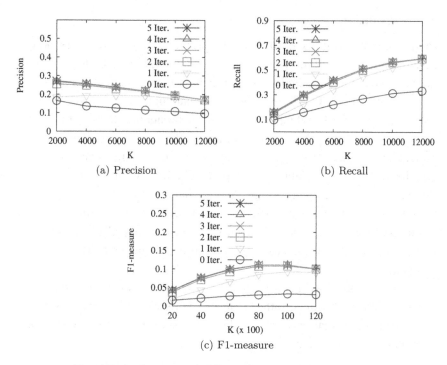

(a) Precision   (b) Recall

(c) F1-measure

Fig. 4.7: Performance of different iterations of CNL$_{LF-E}$.

Table 4.5: Accuracy of NL$_{LF-E}$ and CNL$_{LF-E}$.

Group	NL$_{LF-E}$			CNL$_{LF-E}$		
	100	200	300	100	200	300
Matched	80	142	193	**83**	**151**	**217**
Unknown	18	51	86	17	43	71
Unmatched	2	7	21	2	6	12

As shown in Table 4.5, we find that the accuracy for the top-300 result of CNL$_{LF-E}$ is about 72%, but it is about 64% for NL$_{LF-E}$. This illustrates that both CNL and NL are quite promising in returning the correctly matched user pairs for different top-K ranked pairs. CNL also returns fewer undetermined pairs than NL.

4.7 Conclusion

In this chapter, we have studied the problem of linking users across heterogeneous social networks. It is a challenging task due to large network sizes, heterogeneity in user behavior, and incompleteness and uncertainty in UGC. To handle the challenging task, we propose the algorithm CNL which utilizes the exponential family to model heterogeneous user behavior, evaluates the social similarity in a collective manner, employs LSH to scale up to large-scale network, and handles missing data in E-step of EM algorithm. To the best of our knowledge, this work is the first to handle missing data by using an unsupervised approach. We also evaluate CNL in Foursquare and Twitter networks. Experimental results demonstrate that CNL outperforms existing unsupervised and baseline methods in solving the network linkage problem.

In our future work, we plan to extend the work to link users across multiple networks, rather than two networks since many users are active in many social networking platforms, such as Twitter, Foursquare, Facebook, Google$^+$, etc.

Chapter 5

Quasi-biclique Detection from Bipartite Graphs

In this chapter, we aim to detect a dense sub-structure from bipartite graphs, called *quasi-biclique community* (*QBC*). Compared to the definition of biclique, a *QBC* allows a small number of inter-set edges to be missing. We propose an algorithm, which consists of pruning stage and verification stage, to detect all *maximal QBCs* (*MQBCs*) from bipartite graphs. In the pruning stage, we drive three pruning rules to reduce the sizes of candidate graphs and the number of candidate graphs. In the verification stage, we employ an enumeration tree to enumerate and verify all subgraphs of a candidate graph in a top-down fashion. We have conducted extensive experiments using two real networks to demonstrate the efficiency and accuracy of the proposed algorithm.

5.1 Introduction

Bipartite graph is a very important graph model. In the real world, there are many applications which can be modeled as bipartite graphs, such as rating products and services, watching movies and listening music, etc. Detecting dense sub-structures in such graphs can help us understand user behavior and personalized recommendation, etc. A biclique is the complete subgraph of a bipartite graph (Groshaus and Szwarcfiter, 2010). However, biclique is too strict to be applied in the real world because it does not allow missing any edges between its inter-set vertices, and the real networks are usually dynamic.

In this chapter, we define a dense subgraph in a bipartite graph, called quasi-biclique community (*QBC*). Compared to biclique, a *QBC* is more reasonable since it allows to miss few edges between inter-set vertices. The number of small communities can be exponential to the number of maximal communities that contain them. Thus, if we mine all the small communities, the number of communities will be too large to enumerate efficiently and to output. The above problem is challenging as the maximum vertex quasi-biclique problem is NP-hard (Liu *et al.*, 2008). Hence, computing QBC is also an NP-hard problem because the number of QBCs to be examined grows exponentially with the number of edges. Our objective is to detect all maximal quasi-biclique communities ($MQBC$s) from a given bipartite graph since any QBC must be a subgraph of the corresponding $MQBC$s.

We address the $MQBC$s detection problem using two main ideas, namely: (a) efficient pruning of search space and (b) efficient verification of $MQBC$ candidates. To address the $MQBC$s detection problem, we propose an efficient algorithm called $MQBCD$, which consists of pruning stage and verification stage. We summarize the main research contributions of this work as follows:

- We define QBC, a dense local structure, to model dense community structure in a bipartite graph. Compared with the earlier quasi-biclique (Bu *et al.*, 2003; Abello *et al.*, 2002; Mishra *et al.*, 2005; Yan *et al.*, 2005; Li *et al.*, 2008a; Sim *et al.*, 2006), our defined QBC is balanced in the vertex degree distribution and well connected for inter-set vertices.
- We develop a novel algorithm to detect all $MQBC$s in two stages: pruning stage and verification stage. In the pruning stage, we propose three pruning rules, namely *degree pruning, distance pruning*, and *interaction graph pruning*, to reduce the sizes of candidate graphs and the number of candidate graphs. In the verification stage, we enumerate all subgraphs of a candidate graph in a top-down manner, and construct and verify the associated $MQBC$s.
- We conduct an extensive set of experiments on two real social networks to show the efficiency and effectiveness of our proposed algorithm. We also examine a case of $MQBC$ discovered from the real network.

5.2 Related Work

Uncovering the community structure is crucial to understanding the structure of complex and large networks. Many techniques have been proposed so far. These works in the literature can be grouped into two kinds of community structures.

The first kind considers global community structures. Such communities divide the entire set of graphs into smaller dense subgraphs. The literature offers many global criteria to identify the global communities. Examples are vertex similarity (Leicht *et al.*, 2006), spectral algorithm (Donetti and Munoz, 2004), modularity (Girvan and Newman, 2004; Karrer and Newman, 2011; Ball *et al.*, 2011), and Potts model approach (Ronhovde and Nussinov, 2009) etc. Among them, modularity has been frequently used to evaluate the goodness of community structure of networks. Louvain method (Blondel *et al.*, 2008) is an efficient approach to detect communities by local optimal modularity score. Communities detection for a graph with million nodes using the Louvain method can take only a few minutes.

The second kind involves local community structures. Local community structures focus on subgraphs that satisfy specific local properties, but neglect the rest of the graph. The corresponding structure are mostly maximal subgraphs, which cannot be enlarged by the addition of new vertices and edges without violating the local properties. A clique is defined in a very strict sense as subgraphs whose vertices are all adjacent to one another (Luce and Perry, 1949). In the context of bipartite graph, a biclique is a complete subgraph of the bipartite graph (Groshaus and Szwarcfiter, 2010). Triangles are the simplest cliques, and are frequent in real networks. But larger cliques are less frequent. Similar observation can be obtained for bicliques.

It is however possible to relax the concept of clique, defining subgraphs which are still clique-like structures. The first kind of possibility is to use properties related to the existence of paths between vertices. An *n-clique* is a maximal subgraph such that the distance between each pair of its vertices is not larger than *n* (Alba, 1973). Two other possible alternatives, the *n-clan* and the *n-club*, are defined by Mokken (1979). An *n-clan* is an *n-clique* whose diameter is not larger than *n* (Mokken, 1979; Luce, 1950). An *n-club* is a maximal subgraph of diameter *n* (Mokken, 1979; Jamali and Abolhassani, 2006). The second kind of possibility is to restrict the adjacency of vertices. The idea is that a vertex must be adjacent to some minimum number of other vertices in the subgraph. A *k-plex* is a maximal subgraph in which each vertex is adjacent to all other vertices of the subgraph except at most k of them (Everett, 1982). Similarly, a *k-core* is a maximal subgraph such that each vertex is adjacent to at least k other vertices of the subgraph (Giatsidis *et al.*, 2011; Alvarez-Hamelin *et al.*, 2008). The third kind of possibility is to restrict the density of the subgraph. Compared to a clique, a quasi-clique is a maximal subgraph in which density of the subgraph is not less than a predefined threshold (Abello *et al.*, 2002; Liu and Wong, 2008).

A quasi-biclique is to relax the adjacency of its vertices in a biclique. Bicliques tolerating missing or erroneous data have been studied (Bu *et al.*, 2003; Abello *et al.*, 2002; Mishra *et al.*, 2005; Yan *et al.*, 2005). However, their definitions do not have a good constraint for the vertices to have a balanced error tolerance, thus they often lead to a skewed distribution of the missing edges (Bu *et al.*, 2003; Abello *et al.*, 2002; Yan *et al.*, 2005). To avoid the skewed distribution of the missing edges, Sim *et al.* and Li *et al.* define the absolute and relative versions of quasi-biclique, namely μ-tolerance quasi-biclique (Li *et al.*, 2008a; Sim *et al.*, 2006) and $\delta\%$-tolerance quasi-biclique (Li *et al.*, 2008a). However, their defined quasi-bicliques may not be a connected dense subgraph. In our definition, our defined quasi-biclique can prevent quasi-bicliques from some skewness of missing edges and disconnected subgraphs.

5.3 Problem Definition

We have discussed the bipartite graph in Chapter 2. In this section, we first introduce the concepts related to quasi-biclique community. Then we formally define our problem.

5.3.1 *Basic Concepts*

Given a bipartite graph $G = (V_1, V_2, E)$, V_1 and V_2 are the vertex sets and $V_1 \cap V_2 = \emptyset$, $E \subset V_1 \times V_2$ is the set of edges between V_1 and V_2.

An *QBC* is defined as a dense subgraph in a bipartite graph. The μ-tolerance quasi-biclique is defined in Li *et al.* (2008a).

Definition 5.1 (μ-tolerant Absolute *QBC*). Let V_1 and V_2 be two disjoint vertex sets and $E \subset V_1 \times V_2$ be a set of edges between V_1 and

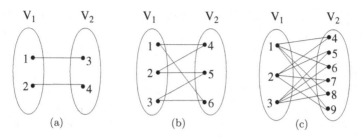

Fig. 5.1: (a) Disjoint QBC; (b) $(1,3)$ absolute QBC; (c) $(\frac{1}{3},3)$ relative QBC.

V_2. $G = (V_1, V_2, E)$ is a μ-**tolerant absolute** QBC if for each $v \in V_i$, $i \in \{1, 2\}$,

(1) v is disconnected from at most μ vertices in V_j, and
(2) v is adjacent to at least μ vertices in V_j[1];

where $j \neq i$.

A μ-**tolerant absolute** QBC does not always look like a densely connected QBC. Figure 5.1(a) depicts a μ-tolerant absolute QBC with $\mu = 1$. Note that the members of each sub-community are not connected and the subgraph does not look like a community. We therefore propose (ϵ, min_size) **absolute** QBC where ϵ and min_size are minimum threshold of missing links and minimum sub-community size, respectively, and $min\_size > 2\epsilon$.

Definition 5.2 $((\epsilon, min\_size)$ **Absolute** $QBC)$. Let V_1 and V_2 be two disjoint vertex sets (or sub-communities), E be a set of edges between V_1 and V_2, and $min\_size > 2\epsilon$. $G = (V_1, V_2, E)$ is a (ϵ, min_size) **absolute** QBC (aQBC) if for each $i \in \{1, 2\}$,

(1) $|V_i| \geq min\_size$;
(2) $|V_j - \Gamma(v)| \leq \epsilon$, for each $v \in V_i$ and $j \neq i$.

(ϵ, min_size) absolute QBC requires each vertex in one vertex set of the biclique to be disconnected to at most ϵ vertices from another vertex set, and the condition $min\_size > 2\epsilon$ ensures that the biclique is

---

[1]Another version of absolute QBC that does not include condition (2) was proposed in a subsequent work (Sim *et al.*, 2006).

connected. The proof of (ϵ, min_size) absolute QBC being connected will be shown in Section 5.5.1. For example, Figure 5.1(a) is not a $(1,2)$ absolute QBC because $min\_size \not> 2\epsilon$. Figure 5.1(b) depicts a $(1,3)$ absolute QBC.

Note that Figure 5.1(b) is also a 1-tolerant absolute QBC. It turns out that (ϵ, min_size) absolute QBC is a special class of μ-tolerant absolute QBC where $\epsilon = \mu$. According to definition of (ϵ, min_size) absolute QBC, every vertex in a vertex set, say V_i, is connected to at least $|V_j| - \epsilon$ vertices in another vertex set V_j. Obviously, $|V_j| - \epsilon \geq min\_size - \epsilon > \epsilon$ because $min\_size > 2\epsilon$. Hence, a (ϵ, min_size) absolute QBC must be a μ-tolerant absolute QBC when $\mu = \epsilon$. As ϵ is an absolute value, it may not work well for large size QBCs. We now introduce the relative version of QBC.

Definition 5.3 (δ-tolerance Relative QBC). Let δ be a small value between 0 and 1, V_1 and V_2 be two disjoint vertex sets (or sub-communities) and E be a set of edges between V_1 and V_2. $G = (V_1, V_2, E)$ is a δ-**tolerance relative QBC** if for each $v \in V_i, i \in \{1, 2\}$, v is disconnected from at most $\delta \cdot |V_j|$ vertices in V_j where $j \neq i$ (Li *et al.*, 2008a).

Similar to the μ-tolerant absolute QBC definition, δ-tolerant relative QBC could be disconnected when $\delta \geq \frac{1}{2}$. For example, Figure 5.1(a) depicts a disconnected $\frac{1}{2}$-tolerant QBC. To allow only connected QBCs, we introduce the (δ, min_size) relative QBC.

Definition 5.4 ((δ, min_size) Relative QBC). Let V_1 and V_2 be two disjoint vertex sets, E be a set of edges between V_1 and V_2, and $\delta < \frac{1}{2}$. $G = (V_1, V_2, E)$ is a (δ, min_size) **relative QBC (rQBC)** if for each $i \in \{1, 2\}$,

(1) $|V_i| \geq min\_size, i = 1, 2$;
(2) $|V_j - N(v)| \leq \delta \cdot |V_j|$, for each $v \in V_i$ and $j \neq i$.

We require $\delta < \frac{1}{2}$ so as to ensure that a vertex is connected to most vertices from another vertex set and the graph stays connected. For example, Figure 5.1(b) depicts a $(\frac{1}{3}, 3)$ relative QBC. By definition, a (δ, min_size) relative QBC must be a δ-tolerant relative QBC.

According to Definitions 5.2 and 5.4, (ϵ, min_size) absolute QBC is also a (δ, min_size) relative QBC when $\delta \geq \frac{\epsilon}{min\_size}$. This is due to the fact that

$$\epsilon \leq \delta \cdot min\_size \leq \delta \cdot |V_j|; \qquad (5.1)$$

$$|N(v)| > |V_j| - \epsilon \geq |V_j| - \delta \cdot |V_j| \geq (1 - \delta)|V_j|. \qquad (5.2)$$

On the other hand, a (δ, min_size) relative QBC may not be a (ϵ, min_size) absolute QBC when $\delta \geq \frac{\epsilon}{min\_size}$. For example, Figure 5.1(c) depicts a $(\frac{1}{3}, 3)$ relative QBC which is not a $(1,3)$ absolute QBC. Moreover, if a vertex set has fewer than three vertices, then ϵ and δ, min_size must be equal to 0.

In our example, the $(\frac{1}{3}, 3)$ relative QBC in Figure 5.1(b) can also be found in another larger $(\frac{1}{3}, 3)$ relative QBC in Figure 5.1(c). Instead of finding all combinations of $(\frac{1}{3}, 3)$ relative QBC, we introduce *maximal QBC* in Definition 5.5.

Definition 5.5 (Maximal QBC). $G = (V_1, V_2, E)$ is a **maximal QBC** (*MQBC*) if there is no other QBC $G' = (V_1', V_2', E')$ such that $G \neq G'$ and $V_1 \subseteq V_1'$, $V_2 \subseteq V_2'$ and $E \subseteq E'$.

For example, the graph in Figure 5.1(b) is not a maximal 1-tolerant absolute QBC because its supergraph is also 1-tolerant absolute QBC. The graph in Figure 5.1(c) is a maximal $(\frac{1}{3}, 3)$ relative QBC if there is no supergraph that is a $(\frac{1}{3}, 3)$ relative QBC.

5.3.2 MQBCD

Given an input bipartite graph, a naive method to return all *MQBC*s is to enumerate and test all subgraphs. The obvious disadvantage of this method is a very large number of candidate *MQBC*s which are costly to generate and test. We therefore propose a framework called *MQBCD* that incorporates three processing steps grouped under pruning and enumeration stages as shown in Figure 5.2.

There are three pruning rules that can be used to reduce the search space. The framework performs Step 1 that reduces an input bipartite graph according to *degree pruning* rule (Rule 1). The main idea is to remove vertices that do not satisfy some degree requirements. Given that

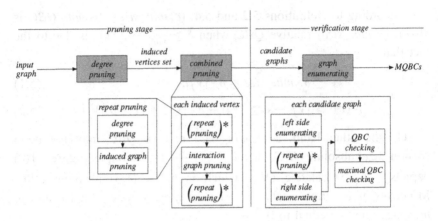

Fig. 5.2: MQBCD framework.

the removal of a set of vertices may change the degree of other vertices, this pruning can be repeated till there are no more vertices that can be removed by the rule. Since each *MQBC* must be the subgraph of an induced graph as shown in Property 2 in Section 5.4.2.1, detecting *MQBC*s of a given bipartite graph is converted into detecting *MQBC*s from its induced graphs. For each vertex in the pruned input graph, we construct an induced graph which consists of a pair of left and right vertex sets. The induced graphs are further pruned using a combined set of pruning rules in Step 2 (combined pruning) before they are used as candidate graphs for computing *MQBC*s in Step 3 (enumeration). These rules will be elaborated in Section 5.4. As we will show later, every *MQBC* is a subgraph of some pruned induced graphs (see Section 5.4.2).

In Step 3 (enumeration), we want to efficiently enumerate all *QBC*s in each candidate graph. The naive approach is to list all subgraphs of a candidate graph and verify if they are *MQBC*s. Even when candidate graphs are smaller, this approach is not efficient because the number of subgraphs in a candidate graph can still be large. So we propose a data structure, called *top-down enumeration tree*, to list subsets of two vertex sets of a candidate graph. After applying the pruning rules possibly repeatedly, we obtain new subgraphs in both left and right vertex sets. These subgraphs are verified to demonstrate the *MQBC*s' properties before they are returned as the final results.

5.4 Pruning Rules

In this section, we present the pruning rules used in Step 1 (degree pruning) and Step 2 (combined pruning) of the MQBCD framework. The three pruning rules used are: *degree pruning*, *distance pruning*, and *interaction graph pruning*. In the following, we elaborate each of these rules.

5.4.1 *Input Graph Pruning*

We first reduce the input graph by removing some vertices and edges that are not required in finding *QBC*s. If a vertex v is contained in a *QBC*, it must have some neighbors connected.

Property 1.

(1) If v is a vertex in an *aQBC*, then $deg(v) \geq min\_size - \epsilon$;
(2) If v is a vertex in an *rQBC*, then $deg(v) \geq min\_size(1 - \delta)$;

where $deg(v)$ denotes the degree of vertex v.

The above properties define the lower bounds of the vertex degrees in a *QBC*. A large number of vertices could be removed as they do not satisfy Property 1. Based on the property, we propose the *degree pruning* rule in Pruning Rule 1.

Pruning Rule 1 (Degree Pruning Rule). Given a bipartite graph $G(V_1, V_2, E)$, we remove a vertex v and its edges if

- For *aQBC*: $deg(v) < min\_size - \epsilon$.
- For *rQBC*: $deg(v) < min\_size(1 - \delta)$.

Proof. According to Property 1, the correctness of this pruning rule can be derived easily. ☐

For example, Figure 5.3(a) is an input bipartite graph and we want to find *aQBC*s with $min\_size = 3$ and $\epsilon = 1$. Using Pruning Rule 1, vertex 13 is removed since its degree is smaller than $min\_size - \epsilon = 3 - 1 = 2$ as shown in Figure 5.3(b). The removal of vertex 13 will cause vertex 7 to be removed as its degree is now smaller than $min\_size - \epsilon$.

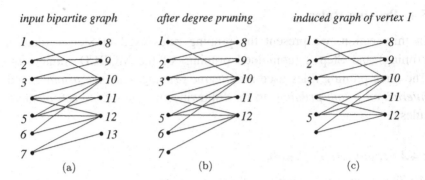

Fig. 5.3: Example of applying pruning rules.

5.4.2 *Induced Graph Pruning*

Every vertex may be a member of a QBC after the above pruning step. Hence, all $QBCs$ can be obtained from combining the $QBCs$ involving different vertices. Let $Q(v)$ be the set of all $QBCs$ containing vertex v in a bipartite graph, then all $QBCs$ in an input bipartite graph can be found in the following set:

$$\bigcup_{v \in V_1 \cup V_2} Q(v).$$

To keep both the set of induced vertices and the sizes of candidate graphs small for efficient computation, we first reduce the size of the set of induced vertices. According to the following lemmas, only vertex set V_1 or V_2 need to be considered as the induced vertex set.

Lemma 5.1. *Let $Q(v)$ and $Q(e)$ be the sets of QBCs containing vertex v and edge e in a bipartite graph, then*

$$Q(v) = \bigcup_{e=(v,u) \in E} Q(e).$$

Proof. On the one hand, for any vertex v and an edge $e = (v, u)$, we obviously have

$$Q(v) \supseteq Q(e).$$

Thus,

$$Q(v) \supseteq \bigcup_{e \in \{(v,u) \in E\}} Q(e).$$

On the other hand, a *QBC* containing vertex v must contain at least one edge $(v, u) \in E$. We therefore have

$$Q(v) \subseteq \bigcup_{e \in \{(v,u) \in E\}} Q(e).$$

Thus,

$$Q(v) = \bigcup_{e = (v,u) \in E} Q(e).$$

$\square$

Lemma 5.2. *Let* (V_1, V_2, E) *be a bipartite graph,* $Q(v)$ *be the set of QBCs containing vertex* v, *then*

$$\bigcup_{v \in V_1} Q(v) = \bigcup_{v \in V_2} Q(v) = \bigcup_{v \in V_1 \cup V_2} Q(v).$$

Proof.

$$\bigcup_{v \in V_1 \cup V_2} Q(v) = \bigcup_{e \in E} Q(e) = \bigcup_{v \in V_1} \bigcup_{e \in \{(v,u) \in E\}} Q(e)$$
$$\subseteq \bigcup_{v \in V_1} Q(v). \text{ (Lemma 5.1)}.$$

That is

$$\bigcup_{v \in V_1} Q(v) = \bigcup_{v \in V_1 \cup V_2} Q(v).$$

Similarly, we can prove that

$$\bigcup_{v \in V_2} Q(v) = \bigcup_{v \in V_1 \cup V_2} Q(v).$$

$\square$

In terms of Lemma 5.2, we only need to detect all *QBC*s induced by vertex $v \in V_1$ or $v \in V_2$. Without loss of generality, for each vertex in V_1, we therefore induce a candidate graph and compute all *QBC*s involving the vertex.

5.4.2.1 *Induced Graph*

We first define for each vertex $v \in V$ in a bipartite graph $G = (V_1, V_2, E)$ three kth hop vertex neighbor sets $S_1(v)$, $S_2(v)$, and $S_3(v)$ based on the distance from v as follows:

$$S_1(v) = N(v), \tag{5.3}$$

$$S_2(v) = N(S_1(v)), \tag{5.4}$$

$$S_3(v) = N(S_2(v)). \tag{5.5}$$

Note that $v \in S_2(v)$, $S_2(v) \subset V_1$, and $S_1(v) \cup S_3(v) \subset V_2$. From the above three vertex sets, we define the following induced graph for computing QBCs.

Definition 5.6 (Induced Graph). Given a vertex v of a bipartite graph $G = (V_1, V_2, E)$, the **induced graph** of v is a bipartite subgraph $Ind(v, G) = (S_2(v), S_1(v) \cup S_3(v), E(v))$, where

$$E(v) = \{(u_1, u_2) | (u_1, u_2) \in E, u_1 \in S_2(v), u_2 \in S_1(v) \cup S_3(v)\}. \tag{5.6}$$

For simplicity, we may represent $Ind(v, G)$ by its two vertex sets $L = S_2(v)$ and $R = S_1(v) \cup S_3(v)$, namely $Ind(v, G) = \langle L, R \rangle$. For the example in Figure 5.3(a), induced graph $Ind(1, G)$ is shown in Figure 5.3(c) and the left and right vertex sets of $Ind(1, G)$ are

$$S_2(1) = \{1, 2, 3, 4, 5, 6\},$$
$$S_1(1) \cup S_3(1) = \{8, 10\} \cup \{8, 9, 10, 11, 12\} = \{8, 9, 10, 11, 12\}.$$

The interesting property of the induced graph is that every QBC is a subgraph of some induced graphs. Before we formally introduce this in Property 2, we first present Lemmas 5.3 and 5.4.

Lemma 5.3. *If vertices v_i and v_j come from the same vertex set of a QBC, then they are adjacent to at least one common vertex in the other vertex set.*

Proof. First, we consider an $aQBC$ $\langle L, R \rangle$. Without loss of generality, suppose that $v_i, v_j \in L$. Both $N_R(v_i)$ and $N_R(v_j)$ have size no smaller than $|R| - \epsilon$. Since $|R| \geq min\_size \geq 2\epsilon$, we have

$$|N_R(v_i)| + |N_R(v_j)| \geq 2|R| - 2\epsilon > |R|. \qquad (5.7)$$

Thus, $N_R(v_i)$ and $N_R(v_j)$ share at least one common vertex.

For *rQBC* with $\delta < \frac{1}{2}$, we can also obtain a similar property as shown in Equation (5.8).

$$|N_R(v_i)| + |N_R(v_j)| \geq 2(1 - \delta)|R| > |R|. \qquad (5.8)$$

$\square$

Lemma 5.4 (Constraint on Distance). *Suppose a bipartite graph* $\langle L, R \rangle$ *is an aQBC or rQBC. For any pair of vertices* $v_i, v_j \in L \cup R (i \neq j)$, *the following constraint holds*:

$$dist(v_i, v_j) = \begin{cases} 1 \text{ or } 3, & \text{if } v_i \text{ and } v_j \text{ come from different vertex sets}; \\ 2, & \text{otherwise}. \end{cases}$$

where $dist(v_i, v_j)$ *denotes the length of shortest paths between* v_i *and* v_j.

Proof. Assume v_i and v_j are from the same vertex set, and without loss of generality, suppose $v_i, v_j \in L$. According to Lemma 5.3, there is at least one vertex, $v_0 \in R$, which is adjacent to vertices v_i and v_j in L. Hence, we have $dist(v_i, v_j) = 2$.

Assume v_i and v_j are from different vertex sets, and suppose $v_i \in L$, and $v_j \in R$. The distance between v_i and v_j is 1 if they are connected. Otherwise, according to definitions of *aQBC* and *rQBC*, there is at least one vertex v_0 in L which is adjacent to vertex $v_j \in R$. Furthermore, according to Lemma 5.3, $v_0 \in R$ and $v_i \in R$ should have at least one common neighbor in L. Thus, we have a shortest path from v_i to v_j with distance $= 3$. $\square$

We can therefore conclude that any pair of vertices in an *aQBC* or *rQBC* are connected by the shortest paths with a distance no larger than 3. Next, we shall state Property 2 as follows:

Property 2. For each vertex $v \in V$ of a bipartite graph G, if it is contained in an *aQBC* or *rQBC*, then the *aQBC* or *rQBC* must be a subgraph of *Ind(v,G)*.

Proof. Let $q = \langle L, R \rangle$ be a (ϵ, *min_size*) absolute or (δ, *min_size*) relative QBC and vertex v be in the QBC. Without loss of generality, let $v \in L$. For any other vertex $v_l \in L$, we have $dist(v, v_l) = 2$. Thus, $v_l \in S_2(v)$.

According to Lemma 5.4, for each vertex $v_r \in R$, we have $v_r \in S_1(v)$ or $v_r \in S_3(v)$. That is to say, $v_r \in S_1(v) \cup S_3(v)$. Thus, the QBC containing vertex v must be a subgraph of $Ind(v, G)$.   □

Based on Property 2, a QBC only involves 3-hop vertices of the induced vertex. Given an induced vertex, k-hop ($k > 3$) vertices can be removed from the input graph in finding all $QBCs$ involving the induced vertex.

5.4.2.2 *Degree Pruning*

Compared to the input bipartite graph, an induced graph may remove the vertices that are far away from the induced vertex. We can therefore apply *degree pruning* rule to prune the induced graph since removal of a vertex affects the degrees of the others. A vertex can be removed from an induced graph if its degrees are smaller than the lower bounds degrees of a QBC. For example, Figure 5.3(c) depicts $Ind(1, G)$, where G is a bipartite graph shown in Figure 5.3(a).

5.4.2.3 *Distance Pruning*

Distance pruning is inspired by the maximum distance between two vertices in a QBC. According to Lemma 5.4, vertices v and u cannot belong to the same QBC if the distance between v and u is larger than 3. The latter situation may occur in an induced graph when some of its vertices are removed from the graph due to *degree pruning*. Hence, we derive the *distance pruning* rule in Pruning Rule 2.

Pruning Rule 2 (Distance Pruning). Let G'_I be subgraph of $Ind(v, G)$ after degree pruning. A vertex u can be removed from G'_I if $dist(v, u)$ in G'_I is larger than 3.

For example, Figure 5.3(a) depicts a subgraph of $ind(1, G)$ after some pruning. According to Pruning Rule 2, vertex 7 is removed from the graph since the distance between vertex 7 and induced vertex 1 is larger than 3. Similarly, vertex 13 is removed from the graph.

5.4.2.4 Interaction Graph Pruning

There is further room for pruning even with Pruning Rules 1 and 2. Consider the input bipartite graph induced by vertex 1 in Figure 5.3(a), $min\_size = 3$ and $\epsilon = 1$. We can get a candidate graph in Figure 5.4(a) after pruning applying *degree pruning* and *distance pruning*. From this candidate graph, we can find only an $aQBC$ $\langle\{1, 2, 3\}, \{8, 9, 10\}\rangle$. There are therefore several vertices that can be removed from the candidate graph.

In terms of Lemma 5.4, the distance of any pair of vertices in a QBC is no greater than 3. For example, the distance between two vertices 8 and 11 in Figure 5.4(a) is larger than 3, i.e., these two vertices cannot be in the same QBC containing the induced vertex 1. Based on this observation, we propose a new pruning rule based on the notion of interaction graph which is defined in terms of the distance between any two vertices from a candidate graph. Before we define the interaction graph, we define the *surviving induced graph* in Definition 5.7.

Definition 5.7 (Surviving Induced Graph). The **surviving induced graph** of vertex v, $sInd(v, G) = \langle L, R \rangle$, is a subgraph of $Ind(v, G)$, if

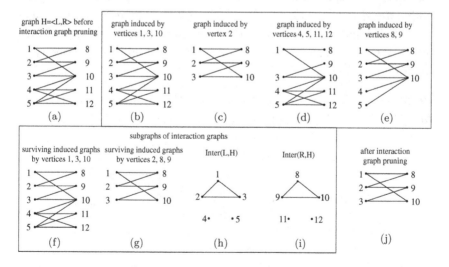

Fig. 5.4: Example of interaction graph.

$v \in L$ and no vertex in $L \cup R$ can be pruned away using *degree* and *distance pruning* rules.

We can easily infer that $sInd(v, G)$ is a super-graph of all QBCs involving vertex v. Based on $sInd(v, G)$, we define the *interaction graph* in the following definition.

Definition 5.8 (Interaction Graph). Let $G = (V_1, V_2, E)$ be a bipartite graph. The **interaction graph** of G, denoted by $Inter(V_1 \cup V_2, G)$, is a graph (V_I, E_I) where $V_I = V_1 \cup V_2$, and

$$E_I = \{(u, v)|v \in sInd(u, G) \wedge u \in sInd(v, G) \wedge u \neq v\}, \qquad (5.9)$$

We call E_I the set of **interaction links**. Specifically, for any vertex set $S \subset V_I$, $Inter(S, G) = (S, E'_I)$ is defined as a subgraph of $Inter(V_I, G)$ if

$$E'_I = \{(u, v)|u, v \in S \wedge v \in sInd(u, G) \wedge u \in sInd(v, G) \wedge u \neq v\}. \qquad (5.10)$$

Intuitively, two vertices are connected by an interaction link in the interaction graph if the distance between them is no larger than 3 and they cannot be removed by another pruning rule. For example, consider the bipartite graph shown in Figure 5.5(a). The graph forms an $aQBC$ with $min\_size = 3$ and $\epsilon = 1$ (or an $rQBC$ with $min\_size = 3$ and $\delta = \frac{1}{3}$). The interaction graph of G is a clique as shown in Figure 5.5(b) as every vertex u can be found in $sInd(v, G)$. We prove this property of *interaction graph* of a QBC.

Property 3. Let $H = \langle L, R \rangle$ be a QBC. Both $Inter(L, H)$ and $Inter(R, H)$ are cliques of size $|L|$ and $|R|$, respectively.

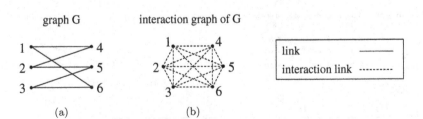

Fig. 5.5: Example of interaction graph.

Proof. Without loss of generality, assume any two vertices $u, v \in L$. According to Lemma 5.4 and Property 2, we have $dist(u, v) = 2$, $v \in sInd(u, H)$ and $u \in sInd(v, H)$ (note that $Ind(v, H) = sInd(v, H)$). (v, u) therefore is an interaction link in $Inter(L, H)$. Hence, $Inter(L, H)$ is a clique of size $|L|$. For the same reason, $Inter(R, H)$ is a clique of size $|R|$. □

With Property 3, all vertices of a QBC in the interaction graph should form a clique of size $|L| + |R|$. For a candidate graph induced by vertex v, we can remove a vertex u from the candidate graph if all cliques involving u do not contain v or their sizes cannot satisfy the *min_size* requirement. Note that finding all cliques and bicliques of $Inter(L \cup R, G)$ is more costly than finding all cliques of $Inter(L, G)$ or $Inter(R, G)$. In our next Pruning Rule 3, we find all maximal cliques of $Inter(L, H)$ and $Inter(R, H)$ to further prune vertices.

Pruning Rule 3 (Interaction Graph Pruning). Let bipartite graph $H = \langle L, R \rangle$ be a subgraph of $Ind(v, G)$ and L contain induced vertex v. A vertex u can be removed from H if

(1) The degree of vertex $u \in Inter(L, H)$ (or $Inter(R, H)$) is smaller than *min_size* $- 1$;
(2) Every maximal clique involving vertex u in $Inter(L, H)$ does not contain the induced vertex v or the clique size is less than *min_size*;
(3) The size of every maximal clique involving vertex u in $Inter(R, H)$ is less than *min_size*.

Proof. Note that induced vertex v is in $Inter(L, H)$. For vertex u of $Inter(L, H)$, if every maximal clique involving vertex u in $Inter(L, H)$ does not contain induced vertex v, then vertices v and u are disconnected in $Inter(L, H)$, i.e., vertices v and u do not exist in the same QBC which satisfies *min_size*. Therefore, vertex u can be removed by finding all QBCs containing induced vertex v.

According to Definition 5.8 and Property 3, only vertices appearing in a maximal clique of $Inter(L, H)$ or $Inter(R, H)$ may be contained in the same QBC. If the size of every maximal clique of $Inter(L, H)$ or $Inter(R, H)$ involving a vertex u is less than *min_size*, then every QBC

contained vertex u does not satisfy the *min_size* requirement. Therefore, vertex u can be removed from H.

Vertex u is not contained in any cliques with sizes no less than *min_size* if its degree is smaller than *min_size* -1. Therefore, vertex u can be also removed from H.   □

This pruning rule says that vertex set of a maximal clique of *Inter*(L, H) or *Inter*(R, H) becomes a candidate vertex set of a *QBC* if its size is no less than *min_size*. Vertices of *Inter*(L, H) are therefore discarded if their degrees in *Inter*(L, H) are smaller than *min_size* -1. The same criteria can be applied to the vertices of *Inter*(R, H). In addition, the maximal clique contains the induced vertex if the former is found in *Inter*(L, H). Furthermore, a bipartite graph may decompose into multiple candidate graphs if multiple maximal cliques in *Inter*(L, H) or *Inter*(R, H) survive after this pruning rule. Formally, let $\{C_i^L\}_{i=1}^{k_l}$ ($\{C_j^R\}_{j=1}^{k_r}$) denote the set of maximal cliques of *Inter*(L, H) (*Inter*(R, H)) after interaction graph pruning. Every pair of vertex sets C_i^L and C_j^R forms a candidate graph $\langle C_i^L, C_j^R \rangle$. We obtain $k_l \times k_r$ candidate graphs. In the remainder of this chapter, the *Interaction graph pruning* rule consists of Pruning Rule 3 and this reduction operation.

For example, bipartite graph $H = \langle L, R \rangle$ induced by vertex 1 in Figure 5.4(a) has 5 vertices in both L and R. We show the induced graphs of every vertex of H in Figures 5.4(b)–5.4(e). It is easy to check that the induced graphs for vertices 4, 5, 11 and 12 do not survive after *degree pruning* and *distance pruning*. Only the graphs in Figures 5.4(f) and 5.4(g) remain. There is no interaction link between vertices 1 and 4 because $1 \notin sInd(4, H)$ after pruning. From these pruned induced graphs, we construct *Inter*(L, H) and *Inter*(R, H) as shown in Figures 5.4(h) and 5.4(i).

According to Property 3, only vertex sets $\{1, 2, 3\}$ and $\{8, 9, 10\}$ may form a *QBC* with *min_size* $= 3$ and $\epsilon = 1$. Hence, we obtain a candidate graph as shown in Figure 5.4(j).

5.4.3 *Combined Pruning Rules for an Induced Graph*

In this section, we combine three pruning rules to iteratively reduce the size of an induced graph as much as possible. *combinedPruning*$(v, Ind(v, G),$

Algorithm 3: Function *combinedPruning*(v, *Ind*(v, G), *min_size*, ϵ)

Input: Induced graph *Ind*(v, G), induced vertex v, parameters *min_size* and ϵ;

Output: *cand*: candidate graph set (initialized to be $\emptyset$);

1 $g_1 \leftarrow$ *repeatedPruning*(v, *Ind*(v, G), *min_size*, ϵ) //integrate Pruning Rules 1-2;

2 *gSet* $\leftarrow$ *interactionPruning*(v, g_1, *min_size*, ϵ) //*interaction graph pruning*;

3 **for** *each candidate graph cand* $\in$ *gSet* **do**

4 | $g_2 \leftarrow$ *repeatedPruning*(v, *cand*, *min_size*, ϵ);

5 | **if** $g_2 \neq \emptyset$ **then**

6 | | *cand* $\leftarrow$ *cand* $\cup$ $\{g_2\}$;

7 | **end**

8 **end**

9 **return** *cand*

---

min_size, ϵ) is the combined pruning operation shown in Algorithm 3, which inputs an induced graph *Ind*(v, G) associated with parameter settings *min_size* and ϵ.

The function *repeatedPruning*(v, *Ind*(v, G), *min_size*, ϵ) at Lines 2 and 5 combines *degree* and *distance pruning* rules together to reduce the size of an induced graph *Ind*(v, G). The function terminates when the candidate graph cannot be reduced further. In the stage of interaction graph pruning, function *interactionPruning*(v, g, *min_size*, ϵ) is performed only once at Line 3 because the pruning rule employs Bron Kerbosch Algorithm to find all maximal cliques (Bron and Kerbosch, 1973) from the interaction graph. The algorithm dominates the major cost in the pruning stage.

The function *repeatedPruning*(v, *Ind*(v, G), *min_size*, ϵ) is shown in Algorithm 4. This algorithm inputs an induced graph *Ind*(v, G) and iteratively removes vertices by employing degree pruning and distance pruning at Lines 5 and 6. It terminates when a candidate graph cannot be further reduced.

Algorithm 4: Function *repeatedPruning(v, Ind(v, G), min_size, ε)*

Input: Induced graph *Ind(v, G)*, induced vertex *v*, parameters *min_size* and *ε*;

Output: Candidate graph *cand*;

1 *cand* ← *Ind(v, G)*;

2 *g* ← ∅;

3 **while** *g* ≠ *cand* **do**

4   *g* ← *cand*;

5   *temp* ← *degreePruning(g, min_size, ε)* //*degree pruning*;

6   *cand* ← *distancePruning(v, temp, min_size)* //*distance pruning*;

7 **end**

8 **return** *cand*

Table 5.1: Complexity analysis in the pruning stage.

Component	Input	Time complexity
Compute induced graph	(V_1', V_2', E')	$O(|E'|)$
Pruning Rule 1 (degree)	(V_1', V_2', E')	$O(|V'| + |E'|)$
Pruning Rule 2 (distance)	(V_1', V_2', E')	$O(|V'| + |E'|)$
Interaction graph construction	(V_1', V_2', E')	$O(|V'| \times |E'|)$
Pruning Rule 3	(V_1', V_2', E')	$O(3^{|V_1'|/3})$ or $O(3^{|V_2'|/3})$

5.4.4 Complexity Analysis

Let $(V_1', V_2', E') \subset G$ be an input graph on which pruning rules are to be applied. Their complexities are shown in Table 5.1. Given an induced vertex, computing the induced graph and the Pruning Rule 2 searches 3-hop neighbors of the induced vertex, and its complexity is $O(|E'|)$. Next, the complexities of computing the vertex degrees in Pruning Rule 1 are $O(|E'|)$. The complexity of further checking degree of every vertex is $O(|V|)$. To sum up, the complexity of repeated pruning is $O(|V'| + |E'|)$.

To construct an interaction graph, we need to compute $|V'|$ induced graphs. Hence, the complexity of computing the interaction graph is therefore $O(|V'| \times |E'|)$. According to Moon and Moser (1965), a graph can have at most $3^{|V'|/3}$ maximal cliques. The Bron–Kerbosch algorithm can be shown to have worst-case running time $O(3^{|V'|/3})$ (Moon and Moser, 1965).

We will further present efficiency of our pruning rules and the whole algorithm using real data in Section 5.7. Even though the complexity of Pruning Rule 3 is exponential to the graph size, it does not take too much time to complete in practice due to the earlier steps. Astute readers may question why we propose this pruning rule. We will leave the answer to the next section that elaborates on the enumeration stage.

5.5 Enumeration of Maximal Quasi-biclique Communities

We now describe an efficient enumeration of all *MQBC*s within a candidate graph. We propose a data structure, called *top-down enumeration tree*, to list all subsets of each vertex set of a candidate graph. We then verify each enumerated graph if it satisfies the criteria of a *QBC* or not.

5.5.1 *Enumeration Tree*

Enumeration tree is a data structure that has been used to list all subgraphs of a given graph (Johnson *et al.*, 1988). For example, Figure 5.6 shows a traditional enumeration tree of a graph with vertex set $\{v_1, v_2, v_3, v_4\}$. Each node in the enumeration tree denotes a subgraph induced by a subset of vertices. The root node is an empty graph and every child node has one more vertex than its parent node. Hence, the ith level of an enumeration tree has $\binom{4}{i}$ nodes, $i = 0, 1, \ldots, 4$. The total number of nodes in the enumeration tree is $\sum_{i=0}^{4} \binom{4}{i} = 2^4 = 16$.

Assume that there is an input graph of n vertices with labels from 1 to n. To avoid duplicates in the enumeration tree, vertices in each node of the enumeration tree are sorted by their labels. Each node w_i in the tree represents a subgraph with i_m vertices, denoted by $\{v_{i_1}, v_{i_2}, \ldots, v_{i_m}\}$. Each child of node w_i extends the set of vertices of w_i with one additional vertex from $v_{i_m+1}, \ldots, v_n$. For example, the subgraph of the child node corresponding to $\{v_2, v_3\}$ in the second level has vertex set

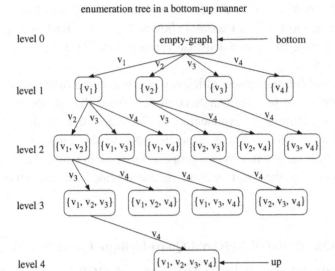

Fig. 5.6: Enumeration tree in bottom-up manner.

$\{v_2, v_3, v_4\}$. A node has no child if it contains vertex v_4. Building an enumeration tree is time- and space-consuming since both the time and space complexities of constructing an enumeration tree for a graph of n vertices are $O(2^n)$.

Enumeration tree can also be used to enumerate a graph. The naive approach for finding all *MQBC*s is to enumerate all subgraphs of the candidate graph. This is however not a scalable approach because the number of possible subgraphs grows exponentially even when no *MQBC* exists with an input graph.

In our proposed approach, we build two enumeration trees, one for each vertex set of a candidate graph. For example, consider the candidate graph in Figure 5.7(b). We enumerate all subsets of vertex set $\{v_1, v_2, v_3, v_4\}$ in a bottom-up manner as shown in Figure 5.6 assuming that *min_size* $= 2$ and $\epsilon = 0$. Such a bottom-up approach has a drawback, which is there are nodes (e.g., at levels 0 and 1) that do not meet *min_size* requirement. We unfortunately cannot remove them from the enumeration tree as their descendant nodes may be *QBC*s meeting the *min_size* requirement.

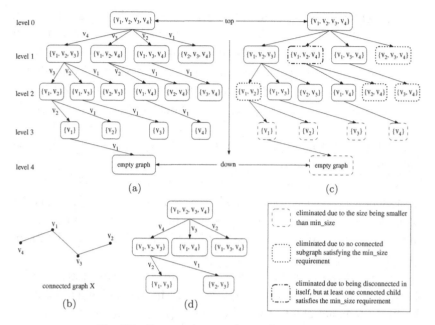

Fig. 5.7: Enumeration tree in top-down manner.

5.5.2 *Enumerating Vertex Set*

To overcome the above drawback, we adopt a *top-down* exploration of the enumeration tree to list all subsets of a vertex set. For example, consider vertex set $\{v_1, v_2, v_3, v_4\}$, a top-down enumeration tree is shown in Figure 5.7(a). The root node is the whole vertex set and every child node is a subgraph of its parent node, which has one more vertex than its child. For example, the subgraph with $\{v_1, v_3, v_4\}$ has a child node with vertices $\{v_3, v_4\}$ after removing the vertex v_1.

We employ the *depth-first search* (*DFS*) to traverse the top-down enumeration tree. The *DFS* starts from the root and explores as far as possible along each branch before backtracking. Formally, *DFS* explores by extending the first child node of the tree and further going deeper and deeper until it arrives at a node that has no child. Note that the first child node always removes the last vertex from its parent node. Then the exploration backtracks, and returns to the most recent node which has not finished exploring. During the exploration, we do not explore child nodes which are children of an already explored node. For example, node

$\{v_1, v_2, v_4\}$ has three subsets: $\{v_1, v_2\}$, $\{v_1, v_4\}$ and $\{v_2, v_4\}$. However, $\{v_1, v_2\}$ is not child of node $\{v_1, v_2, v_4\}$ in the top-down enumeration tree since $\{v_1, v_2\}$ has already been child of $\{v_1, v_2, v_3\}$.

In the depth-first exploration strategy, a vertex set is a leaf-node if it does not contain vertex v_1. We can construct a counter example to prove this. Suppose a node w_i has m vertices, denoted as $\{v_{i_1}, v_{i_2}, \ldots, v_{i_m}\}$, and it does not contain vertex v_1. Consider a child node is obtained by dropping v_{i_j}, and the child node has vertices $\{v_{i_1}, \ldots, v_{i_{j-1}}, v_{i_{j+1}}, \ldots, v_{i_m}\}$. The child node is clearly also a child of $\{v_1, v_{i_1}, \ldots, v_{i_{j-1}}, v_{i_{j+1}}, \ldots, v_{i_m}\}$. In this case, we should not explore the same child node again.

Let *min_size* be 2. Our first observation from Figure 5.7(a) is that all nodes below level 2 have sizes less than *min_size*. Thus, we can eliminate these nodes as shown in Figure 5.7(c). This is a significant advantage over bottom-up enumeration tree.

We now illustrate the process of creating the enumeration tree as shown in Figure 5.7(d) using *min_size* = 2. In the beginning, we check the first candidate child of the root node, $\{v_1, v_2, v_3\}$, by removing the last vertex v_4 from the root node. Node $\{v_1, v_2, v_3\}$ is a child of root node since the number of its vertices satisfies the *min_size* requirement. We next explore node $\{v_1, v_2, v_3\}$. The first candidate child of $\{v_1, v_2, v_3\}$ is $\{v_1, v_2\}$. However, all subsets of $\{v_1, v_2\}$ do not satisfy the *min_size* requirement. We therefore backtrack to node $\{v_1, v_2, v_3\}$ again. In a similar way, the exploration of the enumeration tree continues until all nodes are explored or removed.

In the enumeration process, the left vertex set is treated differently from the right one since we expect the induced vertex to be part of a candidate graph. Hence, subgraphs not containing the induced vertex are eliminated when enumerating the left vertex set. In the end, we only obtain six nodes in the enumeration tree in Figure 5.7(d), rather than 16 nodes shown in Figure 5.7(a).

5.5.3 *Enumerating all QBCs of a Candidate Graph*

Based on the enumeration tree, we presents an efficient way to find all *QBC*s of a candidate graph. The main idea is to enumerate the left and right vertex sets separately.

Algorithm 5: Function *findQBC*(v, $\langle L, R \rangle$, *min_size*, ϵ)

Input: candidate graph $\langle L, R \rangle$ induced by vertex v with parameters *min_size* and ϵ;

Output: Q: all maximal (ϵ, *minsize*) *aQBCs* within $\langle L, R \rangle$;

1   *candLeft* $\leftarrow$ *enumerateSet*(L, *min_size*, "*left*")//enumerating left vertex set;

2 **for** *each node ls* $\in$ *candLeft* **do**

3 | *cand* $\leftarrow$ *repeatedPruning*(v, $\langle ls, R \rangle$, *min_size*, ϵ);

4 | **for** *each* $\langle l, r \rangle$ $\in$ *cand* **do**

5 | | **if** $|ls| = |l|$ **then**

6 | | | *candRight* $\leftarrow$ *enumerateSet*(r, *min_size*, "*right*")//enumerating right vertex set;

7 | | | **for** *each node rs* $\in$ *candRight* **do**

8 | | | | **if** *checkQBC*($\langle ls, rs \rangle$) **then**

9 | | | | | $Q \leftarrow Q \cup \{\langle ls, rs \rangle\}$;

10 | | | | **end**

11 | | | **end**

12 | | **end**

13 | **end**

14 **end**

15 **return** Q

Algorithm 5 consists of three key steps, where enumerating two vertex sets are separated by repeated pruning. At first, the algorithm employs *enumerateSet*(L, *min_size*, "*left*") to construct the enumeration tree, *candLeft*, for the left vertex set at Line 1 such that: (i) the size of each node of *candLeft*(ls) is no less than *min_size*; (ii) ls must contain the induced vertex v. For example, consider the candidate graph $\langle L, R \rangle$ induced by vertex 1 in Figure 5.8(a), and suppose *min_size* $= 2$ and $\epsilon = 0$. Vertex set L has three *QBCs*, ls_1, ls_2 and ls_3. The algorithm generates an enumeration tree *candLeft* containing two *QBCs* ls_1 and ls_2 as shown in Figure 5.8(b), where ls_3 is not a valid node since it does not contain induced vertex 1.

The second step is to reduce the size of subgraph by using repeated pruning. For each subset $ls \in$ *candLeft*, we can get a bipartite graph $\langle ls, R \rangle$. Then, we obtain a set of bipartite graphs by *degree* and *distance* *pruning* rules at Line 3 of Algorithm 5 and store them in *cand*. Any bipartite graph $\langle l, r \rangle$ in *cand* can be discarded if $|l| < |ls|$ since l being a subset exists in the enumeration tree *candLeft* and $\langle l, r \rangle$ can be obtained

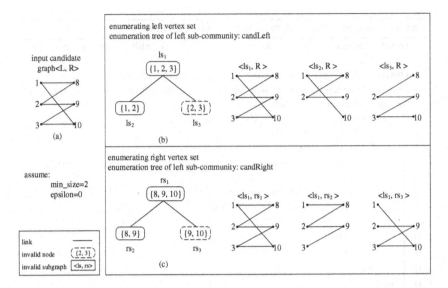

Fig. 5.8: Example of enumerating a candidate graph.

after pruning $\langle l, R \rangle$. In Figure 5.8(b), the algorithm constructs two graphs $\langle ls_1, R \rangle$ and $\langle ls_2, R \rangle$. The graph $\langle ls_2, R \rangle$ is discarded at repeated pruning. Only the graph $\langle ls_1, R \rangle$ remains after repeated pruning.

The final step is to enumerate the right vertex set of a candidate graph, which remains after the second step. The algorithm calls the function *enumerateSet*($r, min\_size,$ "*right*") to construct the enumeration tree *candRight* at Line 6 such that: (i) each node rs is corresponding to a subset of R; (ii) the size of rs is no less than *min_size*. Following the previous example, we enumerate R in $\langle ls_1, R \rangle$, and obtain three QBCs for R as shown in Figure 5.8(c). Finally, we construct three bipartite graphs $\langle ls_1, rs_1 \rangle$, $\langle ls_2, rs_2 \rangle$, and $\langle ls_3, rs_3 \rangle$.

5.5.4 *Verifying QBC*

In the verification stage, for each bipartite graph $\langle ls, rs \rangle$, function *checkQBC*($\langle ls, rs \rangle$) in Algorithm 5 verifies whether bipartite graph $\langle ls, rs \rangle$ is a QBC or not at Line 8. Function *checkQBC*($\langle ls, rs \rangle$) returns true if vertices from both sides satisfy the criteria of QBC. For example, in Figure 5.8, as none of the three bipartite graphs $\langle ls_1, rs_1 \rangle$, $\langle ls_2, rs_2 \rangle$, and $\langle ls_3, rs_3 \rangle$ is a QBC with $min\_size = 2$ and $\epsilon = 0$, the algorithm returns an empty QBC set.

5.5.5 Complexity Analysis

Enumerating a sub-community involves generating all $QBCs$ in the sub-community. Let V be the vertex set of the sub-community. The number of $QBCs$ involving the clique will be of $O(2^{|V|})$. In the worst case, the complexity of enumerating a sub-community is $O(2^{|V|})$. Fortunately, sub-communities are usually small, the probability of forming a clique of large size is very small. Let $\langle L, R \rangle$ be a candidate QBC. The complexity of verifying $\langle L, R \rangle$ is a QBC is $O(|L| \times |R|)$.

5.6 MQBCD Algorithm

In this section, we pull all steps of the MQBCD framework together in Figure 5.2, and propose the MQBCD algorithm in Algorithm 6.

Algorithm 6: MQBCD Algorithm

Input: A bipartite graph G, parameters min_size and ϵ;
Output: Q: the $MQBCs$ set (initialized to be $\emptyset$);

1 $cand\_graph\_queue \leftarrow \emptyset; Q \leftarrow \emptyset$;
2 $G' \leftarrow degreePruning(G, min\_size, \epsilon)// G = (V_1, V_2, E)$;
3 **for** *each node* $v \in V_1$ *and* $|V_1| \geq min\_size$ **do**
4 $\quad$ $v\_cand\_graph\_set \leftarrow combinedPruning(v, G', min\_size, \epsilon)$;
5 $\quad$ **if** $v\_cand\_graph\_set \neq \emptyset$ **then**
6 $\quad\quad$ | add elements of $v\_cand\_graph\_set$ into $cand\_graph\_queue$;
7 $\quad$ **end**
8 $\quad$ $V_1 \leftarrow V_1 \setminus \{v\}$ and remove edges involving v from E;
9 **end**
10 **for** *each element* $v\_cand\_graph \in cand\_graph\_queue$ **do**
11 $\quad$ $v\_QBC\_set \leftarrow findQBC(v\_cand\_graph, min\_size, \epsilon)$;
12 $\quad$ **for** *each* $q \in v\_QBC\_set$ **do**
13 $\quad\quad$ **if** q *does not have supergraph in both* v_QBC_set *and* Q **then**
14 $\quad\quad\quad$ $Q \leftarrow Q \cup \{q\}$;
15 $\quad\quad\quad$ for each $q_1 \in Q$ is induced by vertex v and is a subgraph of q then remove q_1 from Q;
16 $\quad\quad$ **end**
17 $\quad$ **end**
18 **end**
19 **return** Q

5.6.1 Outline of the Algorithm

The MQBCD algorithm requires parameters *min_size* and ϵ. Note that, unless otherwise specified, we just find all the maximal *aQBC*s as the algorithm maximal *rQBC*s can be obtained by a minor change to degree pruning rule in the pruning stage and the criteria to verify *rQBC*s in the verification stage.

Algorithm 6 consists of two stages: pruning stage (from Lines 2 to 9, where Line 2 is *degree pruning* for input graph and Line 4 is the *combined pruning* for each induced graph) and verification stage (from Lines 10 to 18, where Line 11 enumerates all *QBC*s involving vertex v and Lines 12 to 17 verify if a *QBC* forms a *MQBC*).

In the pruning stage, we get the induced vertex set contained in graph G' after applying *degree pruning* rule at Line 2. For each candidate vertex $v \in V_1$, we apply the three pruning rules on the induced graph of v at Line 4. To eliminate duplicates of candidate subgraph, we remove vertex v from V_1 after pruning operation on all candidate graphs which contain vertex v, and update a graph G' in the Line 8.

In the enumeration stage, for each candidate graph *v_cand_graph* that is induced by vertex v, the algorithm finds all *QBC*s involving induced vertex v, denoted as *v_QBC_set*, at Line 11.

For each *QBC* $q \in$ *v_QBC_set*, we add it into Q at Line 14 if its supergraph does not exist in both the result sets Q and *v_QBC_set*. Furthermore, each existing *QBC* in Q, q_1, is removed from Q at Line 15 if q_1 is also induced by vertex v and is a subgraph of q. Note that q_1 cannot become a subgraph of q if q_1 and q have different induced vertices because the induced vertex of q_1 would have been removed before we generate the candidate graph *v_cand_graph* at Line 8.

For each *QBC* $q \in$ *v_QBC_set*, we add it into Q at Line 14 if its supergraph does not exist in both the result sets Q and *v_QBC_set*. Furthermore, each existing *QBC* in Q, q_1, is removed from Q at Line 15 if q_1 is also induced by vertex v and is a subgraph of q. Note that q_1 cannot become a subgraph of q if q_1 and q have different induced vertices because the induced vertex of q_1 would have been removed before we generate the candidate graph *v_cand_graph* at Line 8.

The complexities of the *degree pruning rule*, the *combined pruning* and finding QBCs have been analyzed in previous two sections. Assume that the number of QBCs of an original bipartite graph is N and the maximum size of QBCs is M. Then, the complexity of verifying $MQBC$s from Lines 12 to 17 in Algorithm 6 is $O(MN^2)$ in the worst case when all QBCs share the same induced vertex.

5.7 Experiments

In this section, we evaluate both the efficiency and accuracy of our proposed MQBCD algorithm on two real social networks: Epinions and DBLP. All programs were implemented in Java and were conducted on an Intel core processor with i5-3G CPU and 4GB of RAM.

5.7.1 *Datasets and Settings*

Epinions is a product review website. Users can write subjective reviews about many different types of items, such as software, movies, and videos, etc. A bipartite graph is defined among these Epinion users when the distrust links are ignored (Leskovec *et al.*, 2010). We download the network from the Stanford large network dataset collection.[2]

DBLP is a collaboration network, which records the collaboration relationships. A link is formed between a researcher and a paper if the researcher is a coauthor of the paper. We downloaded the network from DBLP website.[3]

The descriptive statistics of Epinions and DBLP are shown in Table 5.2. Epinions consists of 3,226,975 vertices and 5,954,524 edges.

Table 5.2: The descriptive statistics of Epinions and DBLP networks.

Data	Vertices	Edges
Epinions	3,226,975	5,954,524
DBLP	131,828	841,372

---

[2]http://snap.stanford.edu/data/soc-sign-epinions.html
[3]http://dblp.uni-trier.de/

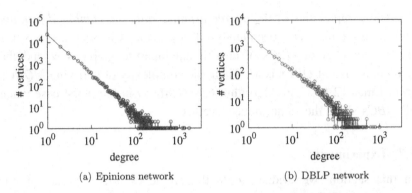

(a) Epinions network   (b) DBLP network

Fig. 5.9: Degree distributions of Epinions and DBLP networks.

And DBLP consists of 131,828 vertices and 841,372 edges. Figure 5.9 illustrates the degree distributions of Epinions and DBLP networks. We found that both Epinions and DBLP networks follow the power law distributions. Unless otherwise specified, the default parameter settings are $min\_size = 3$, $\epsilon = 1$, and $\delta = \frac{1}{3}$.

5.7.2 *Performance Results of MQBCD*

We evaluate two sets of experiments, one for evaluating the absolute version of MQBCD finding $aQBCs$, and the other for $rQBCs$. We denote the absolute and relative versions as aMQBCD and rMQBCD, respectively.

Performance by varying min_size. Figures 5.10(a) and 5.10(c) demonstrate the elapsed time by varying the parameters min_size on both Epinions and DBLP networks. Figures 5.10(b) and 5.10(d) illustrate the number of $aMQBCs$ found from both Epinions and DBLP networks. In summary, aMQBCD takes about a minute to detect all $aMQBCs$ for $min\_size = 3$ and $\epsilon = 0$, but much less time when $min\_size > 3$. This is due to the fact that large value of min_size indicates the large upper bound of vertices, but real networks are scale-free graphs, i.e., only small proportion of vertices have large degrees.

To better understand our proposed algorithm, Figure 5.11 demonstrates the pruning efficiency of aMQBCD by varying min_size and ϵ on Epinions network. The figure illustrates that: (1) almost half of vertices are removed from the input bipartite graph via employing the degree

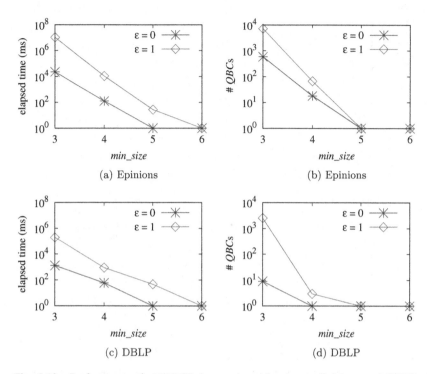

Fig. 5.10:   Performance of aMQBCD by varying *min_size* on Epinions and DBLP.

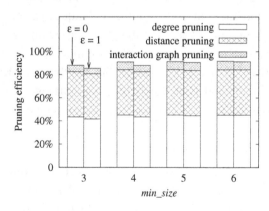

Fig. 5.11:   Pruning efficiency by varying *min_size*.

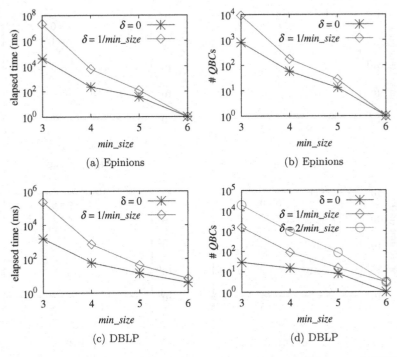

Fig. 5.12: Performance of rMQBCD by varying *min_size* on Epinions and DBLP.

pruning rule, (2) about 90% vertices are removed after pruning stage. We therefore conclude that our pruning techniques perform well.

Figures 5.12(a) and 5.12(c) illustrate the elapsed time of rMQBCD by varying the parameters *min_size* on both Epinions and DBLP networks. Figures 5.12(b) and 5.12(d) illustrate the number of *rMQBCs* found from both Epinions and DBLP networks. Comparing with performance of aMQBCD in Figure 5.10, we can find the similar observations.

5.7.3 *Comparison with Baseline*

MQBminer is an algorithm proposed to detect the noise tolerance of maximal quasi-bicliques from a bipartite network (Sim *et al.*, 2009; Li *et al.*, 2008b). The defined quasi-biclique, which is similar to our defined *MQBCs*, allows every vertex to tolerate up to the same number, or the same percentage, of missing edges. However, their defined *QBCs* may be a disconnected graph when the number of missing edges is large.

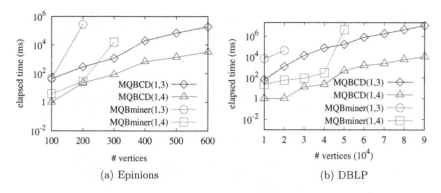

(a) Epinions (b) DBLP

Fig. 5.13: MQBCD vs. baseline.

To illustrate the efficiency of our proposed algorithm, we compare MQBminer with MQBCD. Figure 5.13 illustrates the comparing results. On both Epinions and DBLP networks, the efficiency of MQBCD outperforms that of MQBminer. As shown in Figure 5.11, it may be due to the fact that we employ the distance pruning rule to further reduce both the sizes and the number of candidate networks. However, the distance pruning rule may not be true for detecting the quasi-bicliques defined in Sim *et al.* (2009) and Li *et al.* (2008b) since the quasi-bicliques may not be connected when ϵ is larger than half of *min_size*.

5.7.4 *Case Study*

To gain better understanding of the defined QBC, we conduct the case study in this subsection.

Figure 5.14 demonstrates a found QBC from the DBLP dataset. The left side and right side of the QBC are researchers and papers, respectively. A link is formed if the researcher is a coauthor of the paper. The six researchers worked at University of Pennsylvania. Their research fields are Architecture, Computer Science, and Network Communication. They have the common research interest on Alzheimer's Disease. The four papers listed in the right side are their published papers in the research topic. However, the QBC is not a biclique since "Carlos García Puntonet" is not a coauthor of paper p_4. While they are interested in the research topic for diagnosing Alzheimer's Disease. Thus, we can

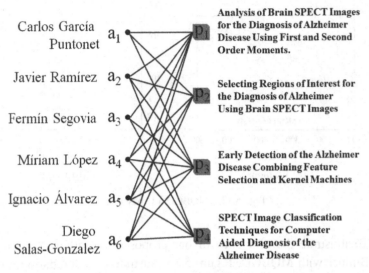

Fig. 5.14: A *QBC* found in DBLP dataset.

conclude that our defined *QBC* is meaningful and useful to mine the local community structures from bipartite graphs.

5.8 Conclusion

The importance of local structures in a graph has been recognized in many application areas, such as understanding user behavior and predicting links between users.

In this chapter, we present a comprehensive study of finding maximal quasi-biclique communities (*MQBCs*) from bipartite graphs. We define both the absolute and relative versions of *QBCs* and propose a two-stage MQBCD algorithm to find all *MQBCs*: pruning and enumeration stages. In the pruning stage, we introduce three pruning rules to reduce the number and sizes of candidate graphs. The experimental results indicate that our pruning rules have high pruning efficiency. In the enumeration stage, we propose an enumeration tree in a top-down manner to enumerate all *QBCs* of each vertex set of a candidate graph. We conduct an extensive set of experiments on real networks. Our results show that MQBCD can efficiently handle an input bipartite graph with hundreds of thousands of vertices and millions of edges.

Chapter 6

On Detecting Antagonistic Community Detection from Signed Graphs

In this chapter, we define a dense sub-structure in a signed graph, called *quasi-antagonistic communities* (*QAC*s) (Gao *et al.*, 2016). Instead of requiring complete set of negative links across its groups, a *QAC* allows a small number of inter-group negative links to be missing. We propose an algorithm, MASCOT, to find all *maximal quasi-antagonistic communities* (*MQAC*s). MASCOT consists of two stages: pruning and enumeration. Based on the properties of *QAC*, we propose four pruning rules to reduce the size of candidate graphs in the pruning stage. We use an enumeration tree to enumerate all *strongly connected subgraphs* in a top-down fashion in the second stage before they are used to construct *MQAC*s. We have conducted extensive experiments using synthetic signed graphs and two real networks to demonstrate the efficiency and accuracy of the MASCOT algorithm. We have also found that detecting *MQAC*s helps us to predict the signs of links.

6.1 Introduction

6.1.1 *Motivation*

The recent surge of online social networks and social media has radically changed the way social communities are studied. Traditional social science research defines social community to be a tightly knit group of users in a social network of friendship links. In the last several decades, researchers have introduced several community definitions each with a distinct criteria for dense connectivities among the community's members. For example, community can be defined as a clique or quasi-clique, or a subgraph that contains much denser internal links than external links (Wasserman and Faust, 1994; Palla *et al.*, 2005). With these definitions, a large body of community detection algorithms have been developed.

In all these above-mentioned research, the common assumption is that there are only positive links among users in the social networks. Many of today's social networks are however signed graphs with positive and negative links. The positive links represent friendship or trust while the negative links represent foe or distrust. Although the traditional definitions of community and community detection algorithms are still applicable to these signed social networks by ignoring the negative links, there are interesting community structures including negative links that should be studied.

In this chapter, we focus on pairs of **antagonistic sub-communities** such that users of the same sub-community share many positive relationships with one another, while users between a pair of antagonistic sub-communities have many negative relationships. A pair of antagonistic sub-communities may represent two political fractions (e.g., republicans vs. democrats), supporters of two rival product brands (e.g., Apple vs. Samsung), or fans of two competing artists (e.g., Justin Bieber vs. Conor Maynard).[1] In these examples, users within the same sub-community enjoy positive relationships among themselves, while users from opposing sub-communities are likely to have negative relationships. Figure 6.1 depicts an example pair of antagonistic sub-communities, $\{u_1, u_2, u_3\}$ and $\{u_4, u_5, u_6\}$.

Antagonistic sub-communities in signed networks have not been studied much in the social science research literature. In the context of signed network, the Social Balance Theory says that for any three users in triadic relationships, their triad is balanced when either only positive relationships exist among them, or one of them has negative relationships with the remaining two users who are positively related as shown in

---

[1]Justin Bieber and Conor Maynard are two teens who enjoy wide success in their singing career.

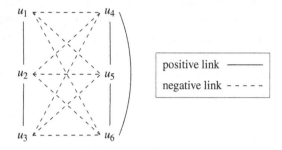

Fig. 6.1:   An antagonistic community.

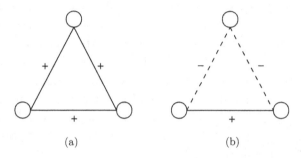

Fig. 6.2:   Balanced triads.

Figure 6.2. A complete signed network therefore has exactly two user groups emerging when all users attempt to reduce cognitive dissonance among themselves by selecting the appropriate signs for their links with other users (Heider, 1946; Cartwright and Harary, 1956). Every user of a group will then have a positive link with every other user in the same group, but a negative link with every user from the other group. As most social networks are not complete, the above scenario can rarely be observed. Nevertheless, if the Social Balance theory is applied to only parts of a social network, one should find multiple pairs of antagonistic user groups in the network.

In this paper, we are therefore interested to find the antagonistic sub-communities as the localized effect of Social Balance theory. The sub-community level hostility may prevent the users across sub-communities from good collaboration and friendly interaction. The interaction among the members from opposing sub-communities may largely focus on topics that are contentious. The antagonistic user sub-communities can also have impact on their neighborhoods as more users may decide to join the antagonism. Given these negative implications, it becomes an important research task to discover antagonistic sub-communities and to intervene in them as early as possible.

Beyond detecting them, one could use antagonistic sub-communities to predict link polarity, user preferences, and product adoption. In link prediction, the balanced triads in antagonistic sub-communities can be used to predict the link polarity (Heider, 1946; Cartwright and Harary, 1956). For user preference and product adoption prediction, antagonistic sub-communities can be used to infer the user preferences as the intra-community users of antagonistic sub-communities are more likely to share similar preferences. For example, Apple and Windows users might be antagonistic to one another, and thus they have different preferences in the products that they purchase or adopt. To the best of our knowledge, exploiting antagonistic sub-communities for predicting polarity, user preferences, and product adoption is an entirely unexplored research territory. The obvious reason here is the lack of prior work on antagonistic sub-communities.

An antagonistic sub-community is a local community structure as opposed to the global community structure that has been studied in many previous community discovery research (Girvan and Newman, 2004; Karrer and Newman, 2011; Ball *et al.*, 2011; Ronhovde and Nussinov, 2009). A global community structure is an optimal partition of the whole network, where each vertex belongs to at least one community. The partition maximizes some global objective functions, rather than local properties. In contrast, an antagonistic sub-community defines a dense subgraph associated with some local properties. It is therefore a local structure. For example, Figure 6.3 shows a network where there is an antagonistic sub-community (in dashed circle) involving vertices v_4, v_5, v_6, v_7 and these vertices belong to two global communities (in solid circle).

The previous works on antagonistic communities can be divided into *indirect* (Zhang *et al.*, 2010, 2013) and *direct* (Lo *et al.*, 2013, 2011) antagonistic sub-communities. The former is applicable to user-rate-item

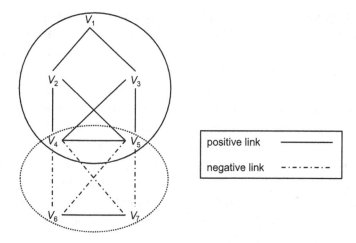

Fig. 6.3: Antagonistic sub-community as a local structure.

where a negative relationship exists between two users when they have significant disagreements in their ratings on some common items. A pair of indirect antagonistic sub-communities involves users of different sub-communities have conflicting ratings on the commonly rated items. Lo *et al.* defined *direct antagonistic community (DAC)* over a signed network (Lo *et al.*, 2013; Abello *et al.*, 2002). A *DAC* consists of two sub-communities. Each sub-community is a strongly connected subgraph with reference to positive links, and the two sub-communities form a biclique with reference to negative links. Due to the sparsity of social networks, missing links between users are very common. However, the biclique requirement is overly restrictive as a user from a sub-community may not interact with every user from the other sub-community. Hence, it is necessary to relax the condition on inter-community negative links.

6.1.2 Research Objectives

In this paper, we introduce a new dense local structure called *quasi-antagonistic community (QAC)* which consists of two connected sub-communities with positive links and two sub-communities form a quasi-biclique of negative links. With this definition, our objective is to detect all *maximal quasi-antagonistic communities (MQACs)* from a given signed network since any *QAC* must be a subgraph of the corresponding $MQAC$s. We only mine maximal communities to reduce the number of mined communities. The number of small communities can be exponential to the number of maximal communities that contain them. Thus, if we mine all the small communities, the number of communities will be too large to enumerate efficiently and output. Furthermore, many of these small communities would be very similar to one another.

The above problem is challenging as the maximum vertex quasi-biclique problem is NP-hard (Liu *et al.*, 2008). Hence, computing QACs is also an NP-hard problem because the number of QACs to be examined grows exponentially with the number of edges. In addition, existing algorithm for detecting DACs cannot apply to find QACs as some members of a QAC may not fully connect to all members on the opposing sub-community.

We address the $MQAC$s detection problem using two main ideas, namely: (a) efficient pruning of search space, and (b) efficient enumeration of $MQAC$ candidates. We summarize the main research contributions of this work as follows:

- We define QAC, a novel dense local structure, to model antagonistic community in a signed network. Compared with the earlier antagonistic community definition (Lo *et al.*, 2013, 2011), QAC is less restrictive as it permits some missing negative links between its two antagonistic sub-communities. We derive two variants of QACs, *absolute* and *relative quasi-antagonistic communities*.
- We develop a novel algorithm called MASCOT to detect all $MQAC$s in two stages: pruning stage and enumeration stage. In the pruning stage, we propose four pruning rules, namely *degree pruning*, *distance pruning*, *strongly connected component pruning*, and *interaction graph pruning*, to reduce the size of candidate graphs to be used for generating $MQAC$s. These rules are all based on the QAC properties. In the enumeration stage, we enumerate all strongly connected subgraphs of a sub-community in a top-down manner, and construct and verify the associated $MQAC$s.
- We conduct an extensive set of experiments on synthetic graphs and two real social networks to show the efficiency and effectiveness of our proposed MASCOT algorithm. We also examine a set of example

cases of $MQAC$s discovered from the real signed networks. In addition, we find that detecting $MQAC$s is helpful to predict signs of links in the signed networks.

6.2 Related Work

Community detection on unsigned networks takes into account only positively valued links. However, many actual networks also feature as signed networks with both positive and negative links. In the context of signed graph, the community structures can be also categorized into the global community structures and the local community structures.

For global community structures, (Doreian and Mrvar, 1996) detect communities from signed networks by optimizing frustration, where frustration is defined by the sum of the number of positive inter-community and the number of negative intra-community links. Anchuri and Ismail propose a spectral approach that tries to maximize modularity and minimize frustration (Anchuri and Magdon-Ismail, 2012). Traag and Bruggeman further extend Potts model by adapting the concept of modularity to detect communities in signed networks (Traag and Bruggeman, 2009). The paper by Mucha and Porter (2010) and Mucha and Onnela (2010) proposed an approach to detect community from arbitrary multi-slice networks, where each slice can be any kind of network. A signed network is treated as a two-slice network: positive slice and negative slice. Correlation clustering is to partition a complete signed network such that it maximizes the number of positive links with clusters, plus the number of negative links between clusters (Bansal et al., 2004). But complete signed networks are very rare in real applications.

The global community structures of a network ignore the local structure of its vertices. The community is significantly different from local community structures, which this paper focuses on. The closest to our work are our previous works (Zhang et al., 2010, 2013; Abello et al., 2002; Lo et al., 2013). Zhang et al. (2010, 2013) proposed an approach to mine antagonistic communities from rating networks. The work focuses on detecting conflicting ratings on some commonly rated objects and determining antagonistic communities from them. Lo et al. proposed an approach to mine antagonistic communities from explicit trust networks (Abello *et al.*, 2002; Lo *et al.*, 2013). The definition of antagonistic community is however very restrictive and does not work well when some links are missing or noisy. In this paper, we therefore define quasi-antagonistic community by relaxing requirement of negative inter-sub-communities links.

6.3 Problem Definition

Our quasi-antagonistic community consists of a pair of sub-communities such that each sub-community is a strongly connected subgraph using positive links, and a quasi-biclique of negative links exists between the two sub-communities. In this section, we first introduce the concepts related to antagonistic community. We then formally define our problem.

6.3.1 Related Concepts

Given an undirected signed graph $G = (V, E^+, E^-)$, where V is a vertex set, E^+ and E^- represent positive edge set and negative edge set, respectively.

Definition 6.1 (Strongly Connected Subgraph). A **strongly connected subgraph (SCS)** of G is a subgraph $G' = (V', E')$ such that there exists a series of edges in G' connecting every pair of vertices in G'.

Definition 6.2 (Strongly Connected Component). A **strongly connected component (SCC)** of G is a strongly connected subgraph that is maximal in size.

Definition 6.3 (Neighborhoods). The **positive neighborhood** of a vertex v in G, denoted as $\Gamma^+(v)$, is defined as

$$\Gamma^+(v) = \{u | (v, u) \in E^+\};$$

We define the *projection of positive neighborhood* of the vertex v to a set of vertices $U \subset V$ with reference to positive links as

$$\Gamma_U^+(v) = \{u | (v, u) \in E^+ \land u \in U\}.$$

The *positive neighborhood of a vertex set S* in a signed graph $G = (V, E^+, E^-)$, denoted as $\Gamma^+(S)$, is defined as

$$\Gamma^+(S) = \{u|(v, u) \in E^+ \wedge v \in S\}.$$

The definitions of *negative neighborhood* and *projection of negative neighborhood* of vertex v, and *negative neighborhood of a vertex set S* are defined in a similar manner.

We define an antagonistic community as a subgraph with two vertex sets densely linked with each other by negative links. Such a subgraph is also known as a **quasi-biclique (QB)** (Li *et al.*, 2008a). Based on the definitions of QBC in Chapter 5, we now define *quasi-antagonistic community* for a signed graph in Definition 6.4.

Definition 6.4 (Quasi-antagonistic Community). A $QB = (L, R, E)$ is a **quasi-antagonistic community (QAC)** if L and R are *strongly connected subgraphs (SCSs)* involving positive edges only.

In this chapter, we consider two versions of QAC, namely the *absolute quasi-antagonistic community* ($aQAC$) if we use (ϵ, min_size) absolute QB introduced in Chapter 5, and *relative quasi-antagonistic community* ($rQAC$) if we use (δ, min_size) relative QB introduced in Chapter 5.

Figure 6.4 depicts an $aQAC$ with (1,3) absolute QB for the negative edges, or an $rQAC$ with $(\frac{1}{3}, 3)$ relative QB for the negative edges. The vertices in each vertex set (or sub-community) form a strongly connected subgraph by positive links.

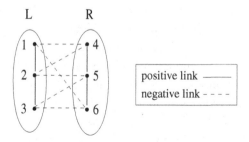

Fig. 6.4: Example of a quasi-antagonistic community.

The above QAC definition relaxes the direct antagonistic community (DAC) in our earlier work (Lo *et al.*, 2011) which requires the negative links between sub-communities to form a complete biclique.

As a QAC may be a subgraph of another larger QAC, we now define the *maximal quasi-antagonistic community*.

Definition 6.5 (Maximal Quasi-antagonistic Community). $H = (L, R, E)$ is a **maximal quasi-antagonistic community (MQAC)** if there is no other QAC $H' = (L', R', E')$ such that $H \neq H'$ and $L \subseteq L', R \subseteq R'$, and $E \subseteq E'$.

For example, the graph in Figure 6.4 is a maximal $aQAC$ with $min\_size = 3$ and $\epsilon = 1$ or a maximal $rQAC$ with $min\_size = 3$ and $\delta = \frac{1}{3}$ because: (1) two sets of vertices are $SCSs$ with reference to positive links only; (2) two sets of vertices form a maximal $(1, 3)$ absolute QB and a maximal $(\frac{1}{3}, 3)$ relative QB with reference to negative links.

Unless otherwise specified, $MQAC$ denotes maximal $aQAC$ or maximal $rQAC$. We also use (L, R) to represent a QB (L, R, E) or a *quasi-antagonistic community (QAC)* (L, R, E) in the remainder of the paper to simplify the notations.

We now define the research problem of our work to be finding all $MQACs$ in a given signed graph. Solving this problem is challenging because the number of $MQACs$ can grow exponentially with the graph size. Therefore, we aim to design an algorithm to find all maximal $aQACs$ and $rQACs$ efficiently. We will present our proposed solution framework in Section 6.3.2.

6.3.2 *MASCOT*

Similar to detecting all MQACs from bipartite graph, we propose a framework called MASCOT that incorporates three processing steps grouped under pruning and enumeration stages as shown in Figure 6.5.

There are four pruning rules that can be used to reduce the search space. In Step 1, it reduces an input signed graph according to the *degree pruning* rule (Rule 1). The main idea is to remove vertices that do not satisfy both positive and negative degree requirements. Since each

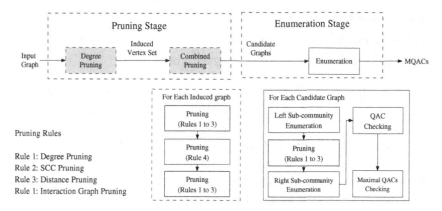

Fig. 6.5: MASCOT framework.

$MQAC$ must be the subgraph of an induced graph, detecting $MQAC$s of a given signed graph is converted into detecting $MQAC$s from its induced graphs. Given an induced graph, it can be reduced by removing vertices in terms of four pruning rules.

In Step 3 (enumeration stage), we want to efficiently enumerate all QACs in each candidate graph. The naive approach is to list all subgraphs of a candidate graph and verify if they are $MQAC$s. Even when candidate graphs are smaller, this approach is not efficient because the number of subgraphs in a candidate graph can still be large. Since each sub-community of a QAC forms an SCS with reference to positive edges, we therefore enumerate all connected subgraphs of each vertex set in a candidate graph. We first enumerates all the SCSs of the left vertex set of the candidate graph. After applying the pruning rules possibly repeatedly, we obtain new subgraphs with SCSs in both left and right vertex sets. These subgraphs are verified to demonstrate the $MQAC$'s properties before they are returned as the final results.

6.4 Pruning Rules

In this section, we introduce the four pruning rules used in MASCOT. They are *degree pruning*, *strongly connected component* (SCC) *pruning*, *distance pruning*, and *interaction graph pruning*.

6.4.1 *Input Graph Pruning*

Similar to Pruning Rule 1 in Chapter 5, we can derive the degree pruning rule for detecting $MQAC$s from a signed graph.

Property 4. Every vertex v in a QAC with $min\_size > 1$ must have $deg^+(v) \geq 1$, where $deg^+(v)$ denotes the positive degree of vertex v.

Taking positive links into account, as each sub-community of a QAC is an SCS, there is a path with positive links between any two vertices in the same sub-community. Thus, the positive degree of a vertex cannot be 0. In addition, each vertex involves a QBC for negative links only.

Property 5.

(1) If v is a vertex in an $aQAC$, then $deg^-(v) \geq min\_size - \epsilon$;
(2) If v is a vertex in an $rQAC$, then $deg^-(v) \geq min\_size(1 - \delta)$;

where $deg^-(v)$ denotes the negative degree of vertex v.

The above properties define the lower bounds of the negative and positive degrees in a QAC. Due to the nature of scale-free networks, both the positive and negative degrees follow power law distribution (Dandekar, 2010; Beyene *et al.*, 2008). In other words, a large number of vertices could be removed as they do not satisfy Properties 4 and 5. Based on these properties, we propose the *degree pruning* rule in Pruning Rule 1.

Pruning Rule 1 (Degree Pruning Rule). Given a signed graph $G(V, E^+, E^-)$, we remove a vertex v and its edges if

- For $aQAC$:

  (1) $deg^+(v) = 0$; or
  (2) $deg^-(v) < min\_size - \epsilon$.

- For $rQAC$:

  (1) $deg^+(v) = 0$; or
  (2) $deg^-(v) < min\_size(1 - \delta)$.

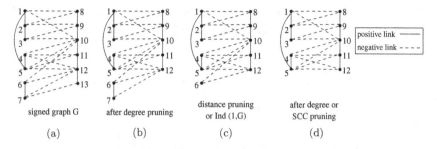

signed graph G   after degree pruning   distance pruning or Ind (1,G)   after degree or SCC pruning

(a)   (b)   (c)   (d)

Fig. 6.6: Example of applying pruning rules.

Proof. According to Properties 4 and 5, the correctness of this pruning rule can be derived easily. □

For example, Figure 6.6(a) is an input signed graph and we want to find *aQAC*s with *min_size* $= 3$ and $\epsilon = 1$. Using Pruning Rule 1, vertex 13 is removed since its negative degree is smaller than *min_size* $- \epsilon = 3 - 1 = 2$ as shown in Figure 6.6(b). The removal of vertex 13 will cause vertex 7 to be removed as its negative degree is now smaller than *min_size* $- \epsilon$.

6.4.2 *Induced Graph Pruning*

Similarly, every vertex may be a member of a *QAC* after the above pruning step. To further reduce the sizes of candidate graphs, for each vertex, we induce a candidate graph and compute all *QAC*s involving the vertex within the candidate graph.

6.4.2.1 *Induced Graph*

We first define for each vertex $v \in V$ in a signed graph $G = (V, E^+, E^-)$ three kth hop negative vertex neighbor sets $S_1(v)$, $S_2(v)$, and $S_3(v)$ based on the negative distance from v as follows:

$$S_1(v) = \Gamma^-(v) \setminus \{v\}, \tag{6.1}$$

$$S_2(v) = \Gamma^-(S_1(v)), \tag{6.2}$$

$$S_3(v) = \Gamma^-(S_2(v)) \setminus \{v\}. \tag{6.3}$$

From the above three vertex sets, we define the candidate graph for computing *QAC*s as an induced graph as follows.

Definition 6.6 (Induced Graph). Given a vertex v of a signed graph $G = (V, E^+, E^-)$, the **induced graph** of v is a signed graph $Ind(v, G) = (\bigcup_{i=1}^{3} S_i(v), E^{+\prime}(v), E^{-\prime}(v))$, where

$$E^{+\prime}(v) = \{(u_1, u_2)|(u_1, u_2) \in E^+, u_1, u_2 \in S_1(v) \cup S_3(v)\}$$

$$\cup \{(u_1, u_2)|(u_1, u_2) \in E^+, u_1, u_2 \in S_2(v)\}, \tag{6.4}$$

$$E^{-\prime}(v) = \{(u_1, u_2)|(u_1, u_2) \in E^-, u_1, u_2 \in \bigcup_{i=1}^{3} S_i(v)\}. \tag{6.5}$$

As mentioned above, we are interested to find the QAC as the localized effect of Social Balance theory. Thus, we remove negative self-loop and unbalanced negative triadic relationships involving the induced vertex from the induced graph in Equations (6.1) and (6.3). For simplicity, we may represent $Ind(v, G)$ by its two vertex sets $S_2(v)$ and $S_1(v) \cup S_3(v)$, i.e., $Ind(v, G) = \langle S_2(v), S_1(v) \cup S_3(v) \rangle$. Formula 6.4 says that positive edges exist in each vertex set, not across the two vertex sets. Meanwhile, Formula 6.5 says that negative links exist between any pair of vertices. For the example in Figure 6.6(a), induced graph $Ind(1, G)$ is shown in Figure 6.6(c) and the left and right vertex sets of $Ind(1, G)$ are, respectively,

$$S_2(1) = \{1, 2, 3, 4, 5, 6\},$$

$$S_1(1) \cup S_3(1) = \{8, 10\} \cup \{8, 9, 10, 11, 12\}.$$

In terms of Lemmas 5.3 and 5.4, we can therefore conclude that the distance between any pair of vertices in a QAC is not larger than 3 with reference to negative links. That is, we have the following Property 6:

Property 6. For each vertex $v \in V$ of a signed graph G, if it is contained in a QAC, then the QAC must be a subgraph of $Ind(v, G)$.

Proof. The property can be proven in the similar manner to Property 2.
□

In addition, there may be vertices duplicated in both left and right vertex sets. This occurs when an unbalanced triangle appears in an induced graph. For example, in Figure 6.7, vertices 1, 2, and 3 form an

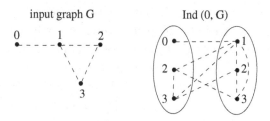

Fig. 6.7: Induced graph with common vertices.

unbalanced triangle. Hence, the vertices 2 and 3 are duplicated in the induced graph of vertex 0.

6.4.2.2   SCC Pruning

Apart from degree pruning (Pruning Rule 1) and distance pruning (Pruning Rule 3) rules mentioned in Chapter 5, each vertex set of a *QAC* must belong to the same *SCC* involving positive links only. We can therefore use the property to further reduce a candidate graph. This is achieved by the Pruning Rule 2 (SCC pruning) below.

Pruning Rule 2 (SCC Pruning). Let the induced graph of a vertex v *Ind(v,G)* be $H = \langle L, R \rangle$. All vertices of an *SCC* can be removed from H if:

(1) The *SCC* overlaps within vertex set L and it does not contain v; or
(2) The size of the *SCC* is less than *min_size*.

We want to extract from *Ind(v, G)* only the *QAC*s containing the induced vertex v. According to Definition 6.6, v is contained in the vertex set L. Therefore, only the *SCC* containing v should be retained. In addition, the vertex set of a *QAC* must be a subset of an *SCC*. As the definition of *QAC* requires each sub-community to have no less than *min_size* vertices, a *SCC* can be removed if its size is smaller than *min_size*.

The first condition of the rule guarantees that every candidate graph generated from an induced graph contains the induced vertex. The second condition says that the *SCC*s in L or R must have at least *min_size* vertices. Suppose $min\_size = 3$, and $\epsilon = 1$. Consider the induced graph of the induced vertex 1 in Figure 6.6(c), vertex 6 can be removed by both conditions because: (i) SCC $\{6\}$ does not contain the induced vertex 1; and (ii) size of SCC $\{6\}$ is smaller than min_size.

In addition, we can partition an induced graph $Ind(v, G) = \langle L, R \rangle$ into multiple candidate graphs $\{\langle C_l, C_r^i \rangle\}_{i=1}^{k}$ if there are k $SCCs$ $(\{C_r^i\}_{i=1}^{k})$ in R with sizes no less than min_size, $v \in C_l \subset L$, and C_l is a SCC with size no less than min_size. In the remainder of this chapter, the SCC *pruning* rule consists of Pruning Rule 2 and this reduction operation.

6.4.2.3 *Interaction Graph Pruning*

Since Pruning Rules 1 to 3 only consider the distance between the induced vertex and another vertices in a candidate graph, there is further room for reducing the size of the candidate graph via taking the negative distance between any two vertices in the candidate graph into account. For example, the negative distance between two vertices 8 and 11 in Figure 6.9(a) is larger than 3, i.e., the two vertices cannot be in the same QAC. Based on this observation, we propose a new pruning rule based on the notion of interaction graph which is defined in terms of the distance with reference to negative links between any two vertices from a candidate graph. Before we define the interaction graph, we define the *surviving induced graph* in Definition 6.7.

Definition 6.7 (Surviving Induced Graph). The **surviving induced graph** of vertex v, $sInd(v, G) = (V', E^{+\prime}, E^{-\prime})$, is a subgraph of $Ind(v, G)$, if $v \in V'$ and no vertex in V' can be pruned away using *degree*, *SCC*, and *distance pruning* rules.

Similarly, $sInd(v, G)$ is a supergraph of all $QACs$ involving vertex v. Based on $sInd(v, G)$, the *interaction graph* can be defined as follows:

Definition 6.8 (Interaction Graph). Let $G = (V, E^+, E^-)$ be a signed graph. The **interaction graph** of G, denoted by $Inter(V, G)$, is a graph (V_I, E_I) where $V_I = V$, and

$$E_I = \{(u, v) | v \in sInd(u, G) \wedge u \in sInd(v, G) \wedge u \neq v\}, \qquad (6.6)$$

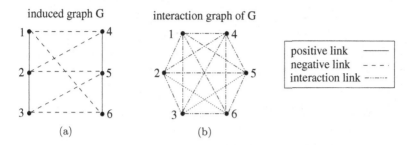

Fig. 6.8:   Example of interaction graph.

We call E_I the set of **interaction links**. Specifically, for any vertex set $S \subset V$, $Inter(S, G) = (S, E_I')$ is defined as a subgraph of $Inter(V, G)$ if

$$E_I' = \{(u, v)|u, v \in S \land v \in sInd(u, G) \land u \in sInd(v, G) \land u \neq v\}.$$

$$(6.7)$$

Intuitively, two vertices are connected by an interaction link in the interaction graph if the distance between them with reference to negative links of a signed graph is no larger than 3 and they cannot be removed by other pruning rules. For example, consider the signed graph shown in Figure 6.8(a). The graph forms an $aQAC$ with $min\_size = 3$ and $\epsilon = 1$ (or an $rQAC$ with $min\_size = 3$ and $\delta = \frac{1}{3}$). The interaction graph of G is a clique as shown in Figure 6.8(b) as every vertex u can be found in $sInd(v, G)$. We prove this property of *interaction graph* of a QAC.

We can derive the same property for the interaction graph to Property 3 and the same pruning rule for detecting QAC to Pruning rule 3. For example, the signed graph $H = \langle L, R \rangle$ induced by vertex 1 in Figure 6.9(a) has 5 vertices in both L and R. We show the induced graphs of every vertex of H in Figures 6.9(b)–6.9(e). It is easy to check that the induced graphs for vertices 4, 5, 11, and 12 do not survive after *degree pruning*, *SCC pruning* and *distance pruning*. Only the graphs in Figures 6.9(f) and 6.9(g) remain. There is no interaction link between vertices 1 and 4 because $1 \notin sInd(4, H)$ after pruning. From these pruned induced graphs, we construct $Inter(L, H)$ and $Inter(R, H)$ as shown in Figures 6.9(i) and 6.9(j). According to Property 3 in Chapter 5, only the

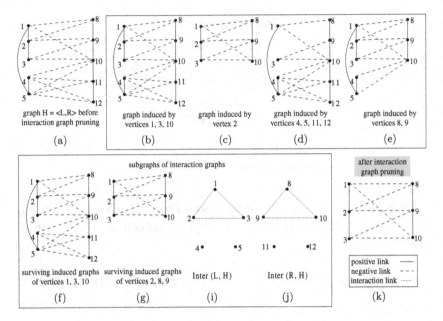

Fig. 6.9: Example of interaction graph pruning.

vertex sets $\{1, 2, 3\}$ and $\{8, 9, 10\}$ may form a *QAC* with *min_size* $= 3$ and $\epsilon = 1$. Hence, we obtain a candidate graph as shown in Figure 6.9(k).

6.4.3 *Combined Pruning Rules for an Induced Graph*

Similar to Algorithm 3, *combinedPruning*$(v, Ind(v, G), min\_size, \epsilon)$ integrates all four pruning rules to reduce the size of *Ind*(v, G). The only difference is that Algorithm 7 may generate multiple candidate graphs after running the function *repeatedPruning* $(v, G, min\_size, \epsilon)$. The function *repeatedPruning*$(v, G, min\_size, \epsilon)$ at Lines 2 and 5 combines *degree*, *SCC*, and *distance pruning* rules together to reduce the size of *G*. The function *repeatedPruning*$(v, G, min\_size, \epsilon)$ is shown in Algorithm 8. This algorithm takes a signed graph *G* induced by vertex *v* and adds it to a queue *Q* at Line 1. The algorithm reduces the size of the first graph of *Q* by degree pruning, *SCC* pruning, and distance pruning at Lines 4, 5, and 7, respectively. Note that an induced graph may break up into smaller graphs after *SCC* pruning since *SCC* pruning keeps

---

Algorithm 7: Function *combinedPruning*(v, *Ind*(v, G), *min_size*, ϵ)

Input: Induced graph *Ind*(v, G), induced vertex v, parameters *min_size* and ϵ;

Output: Candidate graph set: *candSet* (initialized to be $\emptyset$);

1 $gSet_1$ ← *repeatedPruning*(v, *Ind*(v, G), *min_size*, ϵ) //integrate Pruning Rules 1-3;

2 $gSet_2$ ← *interactionPruning*(v, $gSet_1$, *min_size*, ϵ) //*interaction graph pruning*;

3 **for** *each candidate graph* g ∈ $gSet_2$ **do**

4 | $gSet_3$ ← *repeatedPruning*(v, g, *min_size*, ϵ);

5 | *candSet* ← *candSet* ∪ $gSet_3$;

6 **end**

7 **return** *candSet*

Algorithm 8: Function *repeatedPruning*(v, G, *min_size*, ϵ)

Input: Induced graph G, induced vertex v, parameters *min_size* and ϵ;

Output: Set of candidate graphs: *gSet* (initialized to be $\emptyset$);

1 insert G into a queue Q;

2 **while** Q *is not empty* **do**

3 | g ← remove the top graph from Q;

4 | $gCand$ ← *degreePruning*(g, *min_size*, ϵ) //*degree pruning*;

5 | $gCandSet$ ← *sccPruning*($gCand$, *min_size*) // *SCC pruning*;

6 | **for** *each graph* g' ∈ $gCandSet$ **do**

7 | | $cand$ ← *distancePruning*(v, g', *min_size*) //*distance pruning*;

8 | | **if** $cand = g$ // *no vertex in g can be pruned by three pruning rules* **then**

9 | | | $gSet$ ← $gSet$ ∪ {g} //graph g survives after three pruning rules;

10 | | **end**

11 | | **else** insert graph $cand$ into queue Q;

12 | **end**

13 **end**

14 **return** *gSet*

---

one *SCC* of left side and all *SCC*s of right side with size no less than *min_size*. In the implementation, we employ the Tarjan's Algorithm (Tarjan, 1972) to find all *SCC*s of a vertex set. A signed graph *g* is added into the candidate graph set *gSet* if it cannot be pruned further at Line 9. Otherwise, the signed graph is added into the queue *Q* at Line 11. Algorithm 8 runs until no signed graph can be pruned further by the three pruning rules.

6.4.4 Complexity Analysis

Let $(V', E^{+'}, E^{-'}) \subset G$ be the input graph on which pruning rules are to be applied. The complexities of this are shown in Table 6.1. Given an induced vertex, computing the induced graph and the Pruning Rule 3 searches 3-hop negative neighbors of the induced vertex, and its complexity is $O(|E^{-'}|)$. Next, the complexities of computing both positive and negative degrees in Pruning Rule 1 are $O(|V'| + |E^{+'}|)$ and $O(|V'| + |E^{-'}|)$. The complexity of further checking degree of every vertex is $O(|V|)$. The overall complexity of Pruning Rule 1 is therefore $O(|V'| + |E^+| + |E^-|)$. We employ Tarjan's algorithm to find all *SCS*s of a vertex set in the Pruning Rule 2. Its complexity is therefore $O(|V'| + |E^{+'}|)$ [Tarjan (1972)]. To sum up, the complexity of repeated pruning is $O(|V'| + |E^+| + |E^-|)$.

To construct an interaction graph, we need to compute $|V'|$ induced graphs. Hence, the complexity of computing the interaction graph is therefore $O(|V'| \times |E^-|)$. According to Moon and Moser (1965), a graph can have at most $3^{|V'|/3}$ maximal cliques. The Bron–Kerbosch algorithm

Table 6.1: Complexity analysis in the pruning stage.

Component	Input	Time complexity
Compute induced graph	$(V', E^{+'}, E^{-'})$	$O(|E^{-'}|)$
Pruning Rule 1	$(V', E^{+'}, E^{-'})$	$O(|V'| + |E^+| + |E^-|)$
Pruning Rule 2	$(V', E^{+'}, E^{-'})$	$O(|V'| + |E^{+'}|)$
Pruning Rule 3	$(V', E^{+'}, E^{-'})$	$O(|E^{-'}|)$
Interaction graph construction	$(V', E^{+'}, E^{-'})$	$O(|V'| \times |E^-|)$
Pruning Rule 4	$(V', E^{+'}, E^{-'})$	$O(3^{|V'|/3})$

can be shown to have worst-case running time $O(3^{|V'|/3})$ (Moon and Moser, 1965).

6.5 Enumeration Stage

In this section, we also employ the *top-down enumeration tree* to list all *SCS*s of each vertex set of a candidate graph. We then verify each enumerated graph to see if it satisfies the criteria of a *QAC*.

6.5.1 *Enumeration Tree*

To overcome the drawbacks of bottom-up enumeration tree, we adopt a *top-down* exploration of the enumeration tree to list all *SCS*s of a vertex set. For example, consider the same candidate graph $\{v_1, v_2, v_3, v_4\}$ in Figure 6.10(b), a top-down enumeration tree is shown in Figure 6.10(a). The root node is the whole vertex set and every child node is a subgraph of its parent node, which has one more vertex than its child. For example,

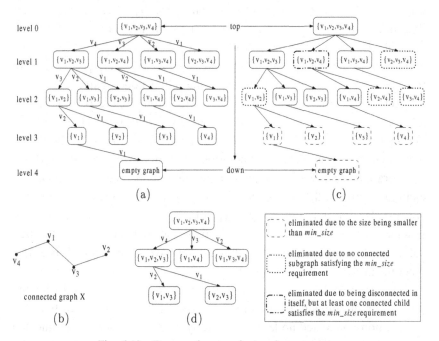

Fig. 6.10: Enumeration tree in top-down manner.

the subgraph with $\{v_1, v_3, v_4\}$ has a child node with vertices $\{v_3, v_4\}$ after removing the vertex v_1.

We employ the *depth-first search* (*DFS*) to traverse the top-down enumeration tree. The *DFS* starts from the root and explores as far as possible along each branch before backtracking. Formally, *DFS* explores by extending the first child node of the tree and further going deeper and deeper until it arrives at a node that has no child. Note that the first child node always removes the last vertex from its parent node. Then the exploration backtracks, and returns to the most recent node which has not finished exploring. During the exploration, we do not explore child nodes which are children of an already explored node. For example, node $\{v_1, v_2, v_4\}$ may have three children: $\{v_1, v_2\}$, $\{v_1, v_4\}$, and $\{v_2, v_4\}$. However, $\{v_1, v_2\}$ is not child of node $\{v_1, v_2, v_4\}$ in the top-down enumeration tree since $\{v_1, v_2\}$ has already been child of $\{v_1, v_2, v_3\}$.

In the depth first exploration strategy, a vertex set is a leaf-node if it does not contain vertex v_1. We can construct a counter example to prove this. Suppose a node i has m vertices, denoted as $\{v_{i_1}, v_{i_2}, \ldots, v_{i_m}\}$, and it does not contain vertex v_1. Consider a child node is obtained by dropping v_{i_j}, and the child node has vertices $\{v_{i_1}, \ldots, v_{i_{j-1}}, v_{i_{j+1}}, \ldots, v_{i_m}\}$. The child node is clearly also a child of $\{v_1, v_{i_1}, \ldots, v_{i_{j-1}}, v_{i_{j+1}}, \ldots, v_{i_m}\}$. In this case, we should not explore the same child node again.

Let *min_size* be 2. Our first observation from Figure 6.10(a) is that all nodes below level 2 have sizes less than *min_size*. Thus, we can eliminate these nodes as shown in Figure 6.10(c). This is a significant advantage over bottom-up enumeration tree. Moreover, in the top-down enumeration tree, we avoid generating non-connected subgraphs. For example, consider the vertex set in Figure 6.10(b), nodes $\{v_1, v_2\}$, $\{v_2, v_4\}$, $\{v_3, v_4\}$, $\{v_1, v_2, v_4\}$, and $\{v_2, v_3, v_4\}$ in Figure 6.10(a) are non-connected graphs. Except for node $\{v_1, v_2, v_4\}$, they and their children in the tree can be eliminated directly since they do not have a child, which is a *SCS* meeting the *min_size* requirement.

However, node $\{v_1, v_2, v_4\}$ has a *SCS* child $\{v_1, v_4\}$ that satisfies the *min_size* requirement. To minimize the size of the enumeration tree, the current non-connected node is replaced by its child, which is a connected subgraph that satisfies the *min_size* requirement. Hence, we replace the node $\{v_1, v_2, v_4\}$ by $\{v_1, v_4\}$. Finally, we can obtain the enumeration tree shown in Figure 6.10(d).

We now illustrate the process of creating the enumeration tree as shown in Figure 6.10(d) using *min_size* = 2. In the beginning, we check the first candidate child of the root node: $\{v_1, v_2, v_3\}$ by removing the last vertex v_4 from the root node. Node $\{v_1, v_2, v_3\}$ is a child of root node since: (1) the number of its vertices satisfies the *min_size* requirement; and (2) it corresponds to subgraphs that are connected. We next explore the node $\{v_1, v_2, v_3\}$. The first candidate child of $\{v_1, v_2, v_3\}$ is $\{v_1, v_2\}$ corresponding to a non-connected subgraph with size 2. Therefore, $\{v_1, v_2\}$ and its children are dropped away from the tree. We backtrack to node $\{v_1, v_2, v_3\}$. The second candidate child of node $\{v_1, v_2, v_3\}$ is $\{v_1, v_3\}$ corresponding to a connected subgraph with size 2. Then $\{v_1, v_3\}$ becomes a child of $\{v_1, v_2, v_3\}$. However, all subgraphs of $\{v_1, v_3\}$ do not satisfy the *min_size* requirement. We therefore backtrack to node $\{v_1, v_2, v_3\}$ again. In a similar way, the exploration of the enumeration tree continues until all nodes are explored or removed.

In the enumeration process, the left vertex set is treated differently from the right one since we expect the induced vertex to be part of a candidate graph. Hence, subgraphs not containing the induced vertex are eliminated when enumerating the left vertex set. In the end, we only obtain six nodes in the enumeration tree in Figure 6.10(d), rather than 16 nodes shown in Figure 6.10(a).

6.5.2 *Enumerating All QACs of a Candidate Graph*

Based on the enumeration tree, we present an efficient way to find all *QAC*s of a candidate graph. The main idea is to enumerate the left and right vertex sets separately.

Algorithm 9 consists of three key steps, where enumerating two vertex sets are separated by repeated pruning. At first, the algorithm employs *enumerateSet(L, min_size, "left")* to construct the enumeration tree, *candLeft*, for the left vertex set at Line 1 such that: (i) each node of *candLeft* is corresponding to a *SCS* with reference to positive links; (ii) there is not negative link for any pair of vertices in the *SCS*; (iii) the

---

Algorithm 9: Function *findQAC*(v, $\langle L, R \rangle$, *min_size*, ϵ)

Input: candidate graph $\langle L, R \rangle$ induced by vertex v with parameters *min_size* and ϵ;

Output: Q: all maximal (ϵ, *minsize*) *aQACs* within $\langle L, R \rangle$;

1   *candLeft* $\leftarrow$ *enumerateSet*(L, *min_size*, "*left*")//enumerating left vertex set;

2   **for** *each node ls* $\in$ *candLeft* **do**

3 | *cand* $\leftarrow$ *repeatedPruning*(v, $\langle ls, R \rangle$, *min_size*, ϵ);

4 | **for** *each* $\langle l, r \rangle$ $\in$ *cand* **do**

5 | **if** $|ls| = |l|$ **then**

6 | *candRight* $\leftarrow$ *enumerateSet*(r, *min_size*, "*right*")//enumerating right vertex set;

7 | **for** *each node rs* $\in$ *candRight* **do**

8 | **if** *checkQAC*($\langle ls, rs \rangle$) **then**

9 | $Q \leftarrow Q \cup \{\langle ls, rs \rangle\}$;

10 | **end**

11 | **end**

12 | **end**

13 | **end**

14 **end**

15 **return** Q

---

size of *SCS* is no less than *min_size*; (iv) each *SCS* must contain the induced vertex v. For example, consider the candidate graph $\langle L, R \rangle$ induced by vertex 1 in Figure 6.11(a), and suppose *min_size* $= 2$ and $\epsilon = 0$. The vertex set L has three *SCS*s, ls_1, ls_2, and ls_3. The algorithm generates an enumeration tree *candLeft* containing two *SCS*s, ls_1 and ls_2, as shown in Figure 6.11(b), where ls_3 is not a valid node since it does not contain induced vertex 1.

The second step is to reduce the size of subgraph by using repeated pruning. For each connected subgraph $ls \in$ *candLeft*, we can get a signed graph $\langle ls, R \rangle$. Then, we obtain a set of signed graphs by *degree*, *SCC*, and *distance pruning* rules at Line 3 of Algorithm 9 and store them in *cand*. Any signed graph $\langle l, r \rangle$ in *cand* can be discarded if $|l| < |ls|$ since l being a connected subgraph exists in the enumeration tree *candLeft* and $\langle l, r \rangle$ can be obtained after pruning $\langle l, R \rangle$. In Figure 6.11(b), the

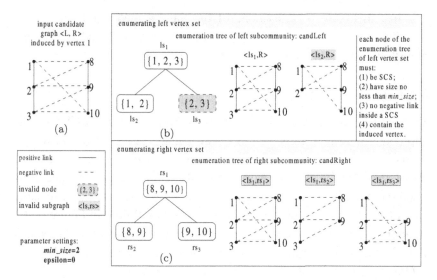

Fig. 6.11: Example of enumerating a candidate graph.

algorithm constructs two graphs $\langle ls_1, R \rangle$ and $\langle ls_2, R \rangle$. The graph $\langle ls_2, R \rangle$ is discarded at repeated pruning. Only the graph $\langle ls_1, R \rangle$ remains after repeated pruning.

The final step is to enumerate the right vertex set of a subgraph, which remains after the second step. The algorithm calls the function *enumerateSet*$(r, min\_size, "right")$ to construct the enumeration tree *candRight* at Line 6 such that: (i) each node rs is corresponding to an *SCS* with reference to positive links; (ii) there is no negative link between any pair vertices of rs; (iii) the size of rs is no less than min_size; (iv) there is no common vertex between ls and rs. Following previous example, we enumerate R in $\langle ls_1, R \rangle$, and obtain three *SCS*s for R as shown in Figure 6.11(c). Finally, we construct three signed graphs $\langle ls_1, rs_1 \rangle$, $\langle ls_1, rs_2 \rangle$, and $\langle ls_1, rs_3 \rangle$.

6.5.3 *Verifying QAC*

In the verification stage, for each signed graph $\langle ls, rs \rangle$, the function *checkQAC*$(\langle ls, rs \rangle)$ in Algorithm 9 verifies whether the signed graph $\langle ls, rs \rangle$ is a *QAC* or not at Line 8. The function *checkQAC*$(\langle ls, rs \rangle)$ returns true if vertices from both sides satisfy the criteria of *QAC*. For example in Figure 6.11, as none of the three signed graphs $\langle ls_1, rs_1 \rangle$, $\langle ls_1, rs_2 \rangle$, and $\langle ls_1, rs_3 \rangle$ is a *QAC* with *min_size* $= 2$ and $\epsilon = 0$, the algorithm returns an empty *QAC* set.

6.5.4 Complexity Analysis

Enumerating a sub-community involves generating all *SCS*s in the sub-community with reference to positive links. Let V be the vertex set of the sub-community. The number of *SCS*s involving the clique will be of the $O(2^{|V|})$. In the worst case, the complexity of enumerating a sub-community is $O(2^{|V|})$. Fortunately, sub-communities are usually small (see distribution of graph size after Pruning Rule 4 in Figure 6.16). In addition, the probability of forming a clique of large size is very small. Let $\langle L, R \rangle$ be a candidate *QAC*. The complexity of verifying $\langle L, R \rangle$ is a *QAC* is $O(|L| \times |R|)$.

Based on the complexity analysis of the enumeration stage, we can better understand the importance and effectiveness of Pruning Rule 4. Note that enumerating a sub-community involves only the positive links of a candidate graph and Pruning Rule 4 involves negative links. Pruning Rule 4 is essential because: (1) the proportion of negative links is small in a signed graph; and (2) the large proportion of positive links in a signed graph affects the number of *SCS*s generated. Further empirical results showing the effectiveness of Pruning Rule 4 will be shown in Figures 6.20, 6.20(d) and 6.14.

6.6 MASCOT Algorithm

In this section, we pull all steps of the MASCOT framework together in Figure 6.5, and propose the MASCOT algorithm in Algorithm 10. We also derive other variants of the MASCOT algorithm which are later used in our experiments.

6.6.1 Outline of Algorithm

The MASCOT algorithm requires parameters *min_size* and ϵ. Note that, unless otherwise specified, we just find all the maximal *aQACs* as the algorithm maximal *rQACs* can be obtained by a minor change to degree

---

Algorithm 10: MASCOT Algorithm

Input: A signed graph G, parameters *min_size* and ϵ;
Output: Q: the *MQACs* set (initialized to be $\emptyset$);
1 *cand_graph_queue* $\leftarrow \emptyset$; $Q \leftarrow \emptyset$;
2 $G' \leftarrow degreePruning(G, min\_size, \epsilon)$// $G = (V, E^+, E^-)$;
3 **for** *each node* $v \in V$ *and* $|V| \geq 2 * min\_size$ **do**
4   *v_cand_graph_set* $\leftarrow combinedPruning(v, G', min\_size, \epsilon)$;
5   **if** *v_cand_graph_set* $\neq \emptyset$ **then**
6 | add elements of *v_cand_graph_set* into *cand_graph_queue*;
7   **end**
8      $V \leftarrow V \setminus \{v\}$ and remove edges involving v from E^+ and E^-;
9 **end**
10 **for** *each element* $v\_cand\_graph \in cand\_graph\_queue$ **do**
11     $v\_QAC\_set \leftarrow findQAC(v\_cand\_graph, min\_size, \epsilon)$;
12   **for** *each* $q \in v\_QAC\_set$ **do**
13   **if** *q does not have supergraph in both* v_QAC_set *and* Q **then**
14           $Q \leftarrow Q \cup \{q\}$;
15   for each $q_1 \in Q$ is induced by vertex v and is a subgraph of q then remove q_1 from Q;
16   **end**
17   **end**
18 **end**
19 **return** Q

---

pruning rule in the pruning stage and the criteria to verify *rQACs* in the enumeration stage.

Algorithm 10 consists of two stages: pruning stage (from Lines 2 to 9, where Line 2 is degree pruning for input graph and Line 4 is the *combined pruning* for each induced graph) and enumeration stage (from Lines 10 to 18, where Line 11 enumerates all *QACs* involving the vertex v and Lines 12–17 verify if a *QAC* forms an *MQAC*).

In the pruning stage, we get the induced vertex set contained in graph G' after applying *degree pruning* rule at Line 2. For each candidate vertex $v \in G'$, we apply the four pruning rules on the induced graph of v at Line 4. To eliminate duplicates of candidate subgraph, we remove vertex v from G' after pruning operation on all candidate graphs which contain the vertex v, and update a graph G' in the Line 8.

In the enumeration stage, for each candidate graph *v_cand_graph* that is induced by vertex v, the algorithm finds all QACs involving the induced vertex v, denoted as *v_QAC_set*, at Line 11.

For each QAC $q \in$ *v_QAC_set*, we add it into Q at Line 14 if its supergraph does not exist in both the result set Q and *v_QAC_set*. Furthermore, each existing QAC in Q, q_1, is removed from Q at Line 15 if q_1 is also induced by vertex v and is a subgraph of q. Note that q_1 cannot become a subgraph of q if q_1 and q have different induced vertices because the induced vertex of q_1 would have been removed before we generate the candidate graph *v_cand_graph* at Line 8.

For each QAC $q \in$ *v_QAC_set*, we add it into Q at Line 14 if its supergraph does not exist in both the result set Q and *v_QAC_set*. Furthermore, each existing QAC in Q, q_1, is removed from Q at Line 15 if q_1 is also induced by vertex v and is a subgraph of q. Note that q_1 cannot become a subgraph of q if q_1 and q have different induced vertices because the induced vertex of q_1 would have been removed before we generate the candidate graph *v_cand_graph* at Line 8.

For example, suppose we have the input signed graph in Figure 6.12(a). Let *min_size* $= 2$ and $\epsilon = 0$. After iterative *degree pruning* at Line 2 of Algorithm 10, MASCOT computes the induced vertex set contained in graph G' with 11 vertices shown as in Figure 6.12(b). For the first induced vertex 1, integrating four pruning rules to pruning $Ind(1, G')$ at Line 4, MASCOT gets one candidate graph shown in Figure 6.12(c). After getting candidate graph induced by vertex 1, MASCOT removes vertex 1 from G' and updates the signed graph G' at Line 8. It is easy to determine that $Ind(2, G')$ and $Ind(3, G')$ can be pruned by combining pruning at Line 4. After removing vertices 1, 2, and 3 at Line 8, we get $Ind(4, G') = \langle\{4, 5, 6\}, \{10, 11, 12\}\rangle$. After pruning vertices from $Ind(4, G')$, we get the second candidate graph shown in Figure 6.12(d). There is no induced graph that can survive after removing vertices 1, 2, 3 and 4 at Line 8.

MASCOT performs enumeration stage from Lines 10 to 18. It enumerates two candidate graphs in Figures 6.12(c) and 6.12(d). For the first candidate graph, there is no candidate graph that can form a QAC with *min_size* $= 2$ and $\epsilon = 0$. For the second candidate graph shown in Figure 6.12(d), MASCOT enumerates the left and right vertex sets by

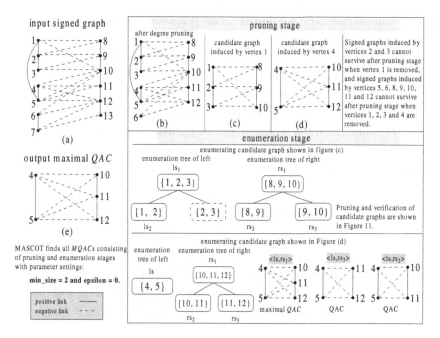

Fig. 6.12: Example of MASCOT.

enumeration trees at Line 11, and finds three QACs $\langle ls, rs_1 \rangle$, $\langle ls, rs_2 \rangle$, and $\langle ls, rs_3 \rangle$ with *min_size* $= 2$ and $\epsilon = 0$. QACs $\langle ls, rs_2 \rangle$ and $\langle ls, rs_3 \rangle$ cannot become $MQAC$s since they are subgraph of $\langle ls, rs_1 \rangle$ at Line 13. Hence, MASCOT outputs $\langle ls, rs_1 \rangle$ as a $MQAC$ at Line 19 as shown in Figure 6.12(e).

The complexities of the *degree pruning rule*, the *combined pruning*, and finding QACs have been analyzed in previous two sections. Assume that the number of QACs of an original signed graph is N and the maximum size of QACs is M. Then, the complexity of verifying $MQAC$s from Lines 12 to 17 in Algorithm 10 is $O(MN^2)$ in the worst case when all QACs share the same induced vertex.

6.6.2   Variants of MASCOT

To the best of our knowledge, there is no other algorithm which finds all $MQAC$s from signed networks. To illustrate the performance of MASCOT and our proposed pruning rules, we therefore propose four variants of MASCOT as baselines.

From MASCOT, we create four proposed variant algorithms as baselines.

Each variant disables one particular pruning rule PR in Algorithm 10, and is denoted by $\text{MASCOT}_{\overline{PR}}$.

In particular, we have $\text{MASCOT}_{\overline{deg}}$, $\text{MASCOT}_{\overline{SCC}}$, $\text{MASCOT}_{\overline{dis}}$, and $\text{MASCOT}_{\overline{int}}$ disabling the *degree pruning*, *SCC pruning*, *distance pruning*, and *interaction graph pruning* rules, respectively. Note that algorithm $\text{MASCOT}_{\overline{deg}}$ disables the *degree pruning* rule in both steps in Lines 2 and 4 of Algorithm 10.

6.7 Experiments on Synthetic Graph

In this section, we evaluate the efficiency and accuracy of MASCOT algorithm on synthetic signed graphs. Given that there are no existing algorithms detecting *MQAC*s, we compare the elapsed time of MASCOT against its variants. All programs were implemented in Java, and run on a dual core 64-Bit processor with 3.06 and 3.06 GHz CPUs, respectively, and 128 GB of RAM.

6.7.1 *Graph Generation*

We first describe our synthetic signed graph generation algorithm as shown in Figure 6.13. Based on a graph generation algorithm proposed by Palmer and Steffan (2000), our algorithm starts with vertex generation, and is followed by edge generation. From the generated undirected graph, we derive a signed graph by assigning sign labels to edges randomly. To evaluate accuracy, we inject *QAC*s into the signed graph in the last step of the generation.

We use *Syn_N* to denote a synthetic signed graph with N vertices. The generator outputs a synthetic graph as shown in Algorithm 11, which

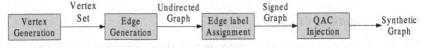

Fig. 6.13: Synthetic graph generation.

Algorithm 11: Synthetic undirected signed graph generation

Input: $N, \theta, \alpha, \beta, [min, max], \epsilon, minDegree(>= max)$;
Output: G: a signed graph injected with some QACs;

1   *vertexSet* ← a vertex set with N vertices;
2   *edgeSet* ← ∅; *totalDeg* ← 0; // initialized sum of degrees;
3   **for** *each vertex $x \in$ vertexSet //Step 1: Vertex generation* **do**
4     $deg(x)$ ← sample an integer value from the power law distribution
     with parameter α;
5   *totalDeg* ← *totalDeg* + $deg(x)$;
6   **end**
7   **if** *numEdge is odd* **then**
8     $deg(x_1)$ ← $deg(x_1)$ + 1; *totalDeg* ← *totalDeg* + 1;
9   **end**
10   sort vertices in *vertexSet* by descending order of $deg(\cdot)$;
11   V ← *vertexSet*;
12   **for** *each vertex $x \in$ vertexSet //Step 2: Edge generation* **do**
13   randomly select a vertex set Y from V s.t. $|Y| = deg(x)$ and $x \notin Y$;
14   **for** *each vertex $y \in Y$* **do**
15   *edgeSet* ← *edgeSet* ∪ $\{(x, y)\}$; $deg(y)$ ← $deg(y)$ − 1;
16   **if** $deg(y) == 0$ **then** V ← $V - \{y\}$;
17   **end**
18   V ← $V - \{x\}$;
19   **end**
20   **for** *each edge $e \in$ edgeSet //Step 3: Label assignment* **do**
21   *random* ∼ $U[0, 1]$;
22   **if** *random* $\leq \theta$ **then** $sign(e)$ ←$'$ $-'$;
23   **else** $sign(e)$ ←$'$ $+'$;
24   **end**
25   *topVertexSet* ← ∅;
26   **for** *each vertex $x \in$ vertexSet* **do**
27   **if** $\min\{deg^+(x), deg^-(x)\} \geq minDegree$ **then**
     topVertexSet ← *topVertexSet* ∪ $\{x\}$;
28   **end**
29   *numQAC* ← $\beta \times N$;

(Continued)

Algorithm 11: (Continued)

30 **for** $i = 1$ *to numQAC* //*Step 4: QACs injection* **do**

31   select a vertex *cand* from *topVertexSet* at *random*;

32   construct vertex sets L and R s.t. *cand* $\in L$, $(L\backslash\{cand\}) \subset \Gamma^+(cand)$, $R \subset \Gamma^-(cand)$ and $|L|$, $|R|$ follow uniform distribution $U[min, max]$;

33   remove all links between any pair of vertices of $L \cup R$;

34   for each vertex set, construct a chain connected by '+' edges s.t. each vertex is randomly assigned its successor;

35     $R' \leftarrow R$; for each vertex $r \in R$, *epsilonR*$(r) \leftarrow 0$;

36   **for** *each vertex* $l \in L$ **do**

37   *epsilonL*$(l) \sim U[0, \min\{\epsilon, |R'|\}]$;

38   *missVertex*$(l) \leftarrow$ randomly select *epsilonL*(l) vertices from R';

39   **for** *each* $r \in missVertex(l)$ **do**

40   *epsilonR*$(r) \leftarrow$ *epsilonR*$(r) + 1$; remove r from R' if *epsilonR*$(r) = \epsilon$;

41   **end**

42   l links all vertices in $R - missVertex(l)$ by using undirected '-' edges;

43   **end**

44 **end**

45 **return** G

---

consists of two parts with eight input parameters as shown in Table 6.2. Note that *minDegree* is degree threshold for selecting vertices to inject *QAC*s. The first part is to generate a signed graph (at Lines 1 to 26). In this part, the algorithm initializes a graph with N vertices and empty adjacency list. To obtain a scale-free network, it assigns a degree k to each vertex v with probability $Pr[deg(v) = k] \approx k^{-\alpha}$. Note that the sum of vertex degree *totalDeg* should be even. The steps from Lines 7 to 9 guarantee this. Next, we assign the neighbors of each vertex after sorting vertices by degree in decreasing order. The final step of this part is to assign positive and negative labels to edges from Lines 22 to 26. Parameter θ controls the required proportion of negative links.

The second part of graph generation is to inject $\beta \times N$ number of *QAC*s into the signed graph (at Lines 27–47).

Table 6.2: Synthetic graph generation parameter settings.

Parameter	Meaning	Value
ϵ	the absolute parameter for $aQAC$	**1**
N	# vertices in a synthetic graph	$[100\,\text{K}, 200\,\text{K}, \ldots, \mathbf{500\,K}]$
β	# QACs per vertex	$[\mathbf{1.0 \times 10^{-3}}, \ldots 1.5 \times 10^{-3}]$
θ	proportion of negative links	$[\mathbf{0.1}, 0.12, \ldots, 0.2]$
α	the power law distribution parameter	$[2.1, 2.3, \mathbf{2.5}, 2.7, 2.9]$
$[min, max]$	minimum and maximum vertex set size constraint	$[3, 8]$
$minDegree$	degree threshold for selecting vertices to inject QAC	**15**

Before we inject QACs into the synthetic graph, a set of vertices *topVertexSet* with both positive and negative degrees $\geq minDegree$ (default value is 15) is selected at Lines 28–30. These vertices are selected to construct QACs since vertices in *topVertexSet* have many positive and negative neighbors. Lines 31–46 of Algorithm 11 inject QACs into the synthetic graph. The injection controls: (1) the number of vertices of each sub-community; (2) the edges within and across sub-communities.

Assume that $Q_{ac} = \langle L, R \rangle$ be an injected QAC. $|L|$ and $|R|$ are two numbers sampled from a uniform distribution $U[min, max]$ at Line 34. L and R are selected from vertex set $\Gamma^{+}(cand)$ or $\Gamma^{-}(cand)$ randomly at Line 35, i.e., $L \subset \Gamma^{+}(cand)$ and $R \subset \Gamma^{-}(cand)$ (Note that $max < minDegree$).

To ensure that L and R form a QAC, the algorithm removes all edges between any pair of vertices in $L \cup R$ at Line 36. A chain of positive links is formed in L and R separately at Line 37 so that each of them is now an SCS. Finally, $\langle L, R \rangle$ forms a (ϵ, min) absolute QB from Lines 39 to 46. According to the definition of (ϵ, min) absolute QB, $epsilonL(v)$, $epsilonR(v) \leq \epsilon$, where $epsilonL(v)$ ($epsilonR(v)$) denotes the number of disconnected vertices of v. In the algorithm, Line 40 guarantees the negative degree requirement of vertices from L, and Lines 42–44 guarantee the same requirement for R vertices. All negative neighbors of a vertex are assigned at Line 45.

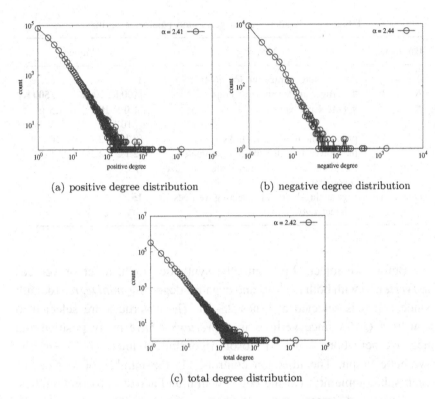

(a) positive degree distribution   (b) negative degree distribution

(c) total degree distribution

Fig. 6.14: Degree distributions of *Syn_*500 K.

Figure 6.14 shows the distributions of positive, negative, and total degrees of a synthetic signed graph generated with $N = 500$ K, $\beta = 0.001$, $\theta = 0.1$, $\alpha = 2.5$, $min = 3$, $\epsilon = 1$, $max = 8$, and $minDegree = 15$, denoted as *Syn_*500 K. We observe that degree distributions follow power law as expected. Unless otherwise specified, the default parameter settings for the generator are listed in Table 6.2.

6.7.2 *Performance Results*

We create two sets of synthetic graphs, one for evaluating the absolute version of MASCOT finding *aQAC*s, and the other for *rQAC*s. We denote the absolute and relative versions as *aMascot* and *rMascot*, respectively.

Measures of performance. We adopt two performance measures: (i) the elapsed time and; (ii) recall, that measure the efficiency and accuracy of the algorithms, respectively.

We measure the elapsed time in seconds, and it consists of the elapsed time of pruning rules and the elapsed time of enumerating candidate graphs. Recall is derived from the number of $MQAC$s found by MASCOT. Every $MQAC$ found by an algorithm may belong to one of three categories below.

- Type I: It is one of the injected QACs.
- Type II: It is a supergraph of any injected QAC.
- Type III: It is not a supergraph of any injected QAC.

An injected QAC is considered found if it is among the found QACs (i.e., Type I), or is a subgraph of some found QACs (i.e., Type II). Therefore, we can define two recalls for Types I and II as

$$recall_I = \frac{\text{\# injected } QAC\text{s that are found based on Type I criteria}}{\text{\# injected } QAC\text{s}};$$

$$recall_{II} = \frac{\text{\# injected } QAC\text{s that are found based on Type II criteria}}{\text{\# injected } QAC\text{s}}.$$

We then define total recall to be $recall = recall_I + recall_{II}$.

Performance by varying graph size N. We evaluate MASCOT algorithm on synthetic graphs of size from 100 K to 500 K. We record the elapsed time of *aMascot* on synthetic graphs injected with *aQACs*, that of *rMascot* injected with *rQACs*, and baselines. Note that we show the elapsed times of MASCOT and baselines in Figures 6.15(a) and 6.15(b) if the elapsed time is not longer than 8 hours, i.e., $\text{MASCOT}_{\overline{deg}}$ takes more than 8 hours to find all $MQAC$s when $N \geq 300\,\text{K}$. As shown in Figures 6.15(a) and 6.15(b), *aMascot* and *rMascot* outperform all baselines and requires less than 60 seconds when $N = 500\,\text{K}$.

We observe that without using specific pruning rules, the baselines may take much longer time. In terms of performance of baselines, interaction graph pruning also appears to play a significant part reducing the elapsed time.

From Figures 6.15(a) and 6.15(b), we also observe that the elapsed time for both *aMascot* and *rMascot* increases as the input graph size increases. To analyze the elapsed time further, we show some descriptive statistics for input graphs with different graph sizes (N) in Table 6.3.

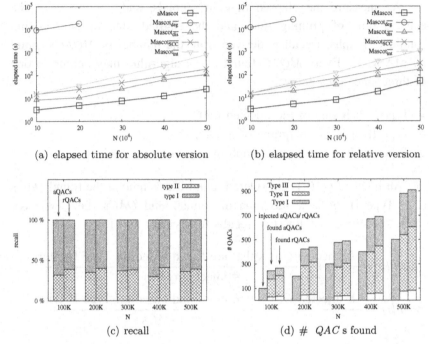

(a) elapsed time for absolute version   (b) elapsed time for relative version

(c) recall   (d) # *QAC*s found

Fig. 6.15: Performance by varying graph size (N) ($min\_size = 3$, $\epsilon = 1$, $\delta = \frac{1}{3}$, $\beta = 0.001$, $\theta = 0.1$, $\alpha = 2.5$).

Table 6.3: Descriptive statistics over synthetic graphs.

N	100 K	200 K	300 K	400 K	500 K
# injected QACs	100	200	300	400	500
|*topVertexSet*|	161	326	495	645	823
QACperVertex	0.62	0.61	0.60	0.62	0.60
# candidate graphs after pruning stage	274	813	1,519	2,644	4,109

The statistic *QACperVertex* is defined by

$$QACperVertex = \frac{\# \text{ injected } QACs}{|topVertexSet|}. \tag{6.8}$$

A larger value for *QACperVertex* implies higher chance for two injected QACs to share the same vertex.

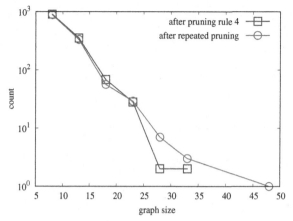

after repeated pruning and pruning rule 4

Fig. 6.16: Distributions of graph size.

As shown in Table 6.3, *QACperVertex* does not vary much with N. Table 6.3 also shows that MASCOT gets more candidate graphs after the pruning stage. This explains more elapsed time for larger N.

To better understand interaction graph pruning, Figure 6.16 shows the distributions of graph size after repeated pruning and applying Pruning Rule 4 on *Syn_500 K*. We observe that: (1) the graph sizes are quite small after repeated pruning; and (2) Pruning Rule 4 further reduces the large graphs to small ones. It indicates the effectiveness of Pruning Rules 1–4. To sum up these results, both *aMascot* and *rMascot* run fast on our synthetic graphs and their pruning rules are very effective in reducing the search space.

Figure 6.15(c) shows the recalls of *aMascot* and *rMascot*. We observe the recalls of *aMascot* and *rMascot* are 100% for different N with more than 50% of injected *QAC*s recovered in their original forms. For the remaining injected *QAC*s, some of the found *MQAC*s are their supergraphs. We therefore conclude that MASCOT has high recall on the synthetic graphs.

Figure 6.15(d) shows the actual numbers of *MQAC*s found by *aMascot* and *rMascot*. For each N, the left bar shows the number of injected *aQAC*s or *rQAC*s. The middle and right bars show the composition of *aQAC*s or *rQAC*s found matching against the injected *QAC*s on the

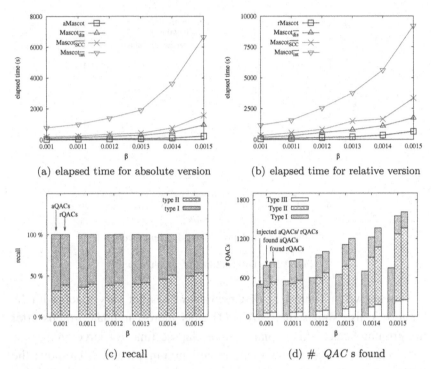

(a) elapsed time for absolute version   (b) elapsed time for relative version

(c) recall   (d) # QAC s found

Fig. 6.17: Performance by varying proportions of injected $QACs$ $(\beta)(N = 500\,\text{K}$, $min\_size = 3, \epsilon = 1, \delta = \frac{1}{3}, \theta = 0.1, \alpha = 2.5)$.

synthetic graphs. From Figure 6.15(d), we observe that only a small proportion of $MQACs$ found belong to Type III. That is, most $MQACs$ are either injected $QACs$ or their supergraphs.

Performance by varying the proportion of injected $QACs$ β. Figures 6.17(a) and 6.17(b) show the elapsed times of MASCOT and baselines by varying β. Please note that MASCOT$_{\overline{deg}}$ takes more than 8 hours to find all $MQACs$.

It is easy to find that MASCOT outperforms all baselines. From Figures 6.17(a) and 6.17(b), we also observe that the elapsed time increases with β. This is due to more candidate graphs remaining after pruning rules, and more injected $QACs$ sharing common vertices as β increases. Figure 6.17(c) shows that the total recall is still 100% suggesting that MASCOT returns all injected $QACs$ in original or supergraph form.

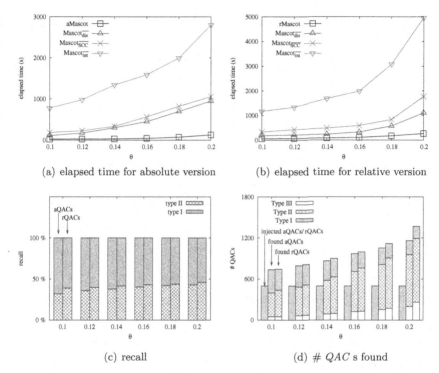

(a) elapsed time for absolute version   (b) elapsed time for relative version

(c) recall   (d) # QAC s found

Fig. 6.18: Performance by varying proportions of negative links (θ) ($N = 500\,$K, $min\_size = 3, \epsilon = 1, \delta = \frac{1}{3}, \beta = 0.001, \alpha = 2.5$).

As shown in Figure 6.17(d), smaller proportions of Type I $MQAC$s are found since the injected QACs share more vertices.

Performance by varying proportions of negative links θ. Figures 6.18(a) and 6.18(b) show the elapsed times of MASCOT and baselines when increasing the proportion of negative links in a synthetic graph. Note that MASCOT$_{\overline{deg}}$ takes more than 8 hours to find all $MQAC$s with different values of θ. MASCOT also outperforms all baselines. The figures show the elapsed time increases with θ. As the proportion of negative links becomes larger, MASCOT has larger induced graphs, thus requiring more elapsed time. Despite that, Figure 6.18(c) shows that MASCOT still achieves very high recall. From Figure 6.18(d), we observe smaller proportions of $MQAC$s found belonging to Type I since the injected QACs are likely to be larger when more negative links are in the signed graph.

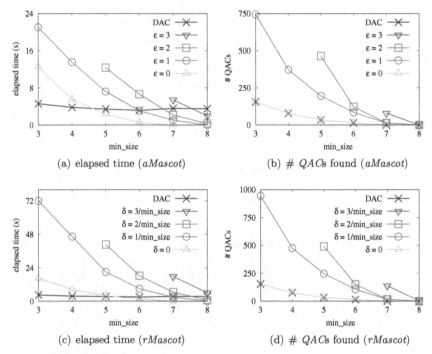

(a) elapsed time (*aMascot*)   (b) # *QAC*s found (*aMascot*)

(c) elapsed time (*rMascot*)   (d) # *QAC*s found (*rMascot*)

Fig. 6.19: Performance by varying *min_size* ($N = 500$ K, $\beta = 0.001$, $\theta = 0.1$, $\alpha = 2.5$).

Performance by varying *min_size*. Figures 6.19(a) and 6.19(b)
illustrate the performance of *aMascot* on *Syn_500* K injected with *aQACs*
by varying *min_size* from 3 to 8. We can observe that the elapsed time
for *aMascot* decreases as *min_size* increases, as does the number of
aMQACs. This shows that MASCOT is able to reduce the elapsed time
and search space using *min_size*. As we use larger ϵ, the elapsed time
increases. A larger ϵ increases the number of *QAC*s to be found, hence
increasing the time required. In Figures 6.20(c) and 6.20(d), we observe
the similar performance trends for *rMascot*.

In addition, we also compare MASCOT with the algorithm for
detecting *DAC*s (Lo *et al.*, 2011) when $\epsilon = 0$ or $\delta = 0$. Under these
conditions, the inter-community negative links of a *QAC* form a biclique,
which is fully connected by negative links; thus, the *QAC* will also be a
DAC. We show the results of our experiments in Figures 6.19(a)–6.19(d).
From Figures 6.19(a) and 6.19(c), when *min_size* is large, both *aMascot*

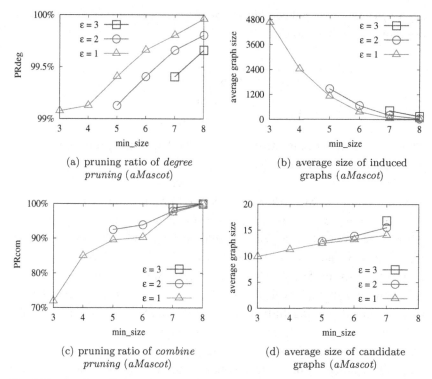

(a) pruning ratio of *degree*
pruning (*aMascot*)

(b) average size of induced
graphs (*aMascot*)

(c) pruning ratio of *combine*
pruning (*aMascot*)

(d) average size of candidate
graphs (*aMascot*)

Fig. 6.20: Pruning efficiency by varying *min_size* ($N = 500$ K, $\beta = 0.001$, $\theta = 0.1$, $\alpha = 2.5$).

and *rMascot* are more efficient than the algorithm that mines *DAC*s. From Figures 6.19(b) and 6.19(d), we observe that *aQAC* and *rQAC* help us to find more antagonistic communities due to their relaxed conditions. Note that the elapsed time for detecting *DAC*s is not affected by *min_size* since the algorithm for detecting *DAC*s generates all maximal bicliques from some subgraphs.

To understand the effectiveness of pruning, we measure the pruning efficiency of our pruning rules. Our pruning aims to reduce the number of candidate graphs and their sizes. We therefore introduce two pruning efficiency measures: (i) average graph size after pruning and; (ii) pruning ratio of each pruning rule. Average graph size is defined by summing the number of vertices of induced or candidate graphs divided by the number of such graphs after applying the pruning rule. The pruning ratio of *degree pruning* rule and *combined pruning* (i.e., degree, SCC and distance pruning) are defined as

$$PRdeg = 1 - \frac{\# \text{ induced vertices}}{\# \text{ vertices in an input graph}};$$

$$PRcom = 1 - \frac{\# \text{ candidate graphs}}{\# \text{ induced graphs}}.$$

PRdeg and *PRcom* range from 0 to 1. The larger the pruning ratio, the more effective is pruning.

Figure 6.20 shows the pruning efficiency of *aMascot* by varying *min_size* and ϵ on *Syn_500 K*. The derived pruning ratio *PRdeg* exceeds 99% which suggests many vertices are pruned away. The average induced graph size after *degree pruning* rule has around 4 K vertices when *min_size* = 3 and $\epsilon = 1$. While this number is small compared with 500 K vertices in *Syn_500 K*, it is still computationally expensive to enumerate a subgraph with thousands of vertices. Figure 6.20(c) shows that combined pruning further reduces the number of candidate graphs with pruning ratio *PRcom* above 70%. Figure 6.20(d) further shows that the average candidate graph size is smaller than 20. We therefore conclude that our pruning techniques achieve good pruning efficiency. The same conclusion can be made for *rMascot*.

6.8 Experiments on Real Networks

In this section, we report the results and analysis of MASCOT for finding all *MQAC*s in two real social networks: myGamma and Epinions.

6.8.1 *Description of Datasets*

myGamma. myGamma is an online social networking site, which can be accessed through mobile phone with an Internet connection. On that network, friendships are considered positive links, and a negative link is defined between two users when one of them blocks the others. In our experiment, we select myGamma users from eight countries in five continents. Some descriptive statistics of this network is given in Table 6.4. The statistic *ratio*$^-$ denotes the proportion of negative links. We remove both positive and negative self-loop edges and directed edges

Table 6.4: Descriptive statistics on myGamma networks grouped by countries.

countryID	Country	# users	# edges	*ratio⁻*	Density
au	Australia	2,325	7,895	0.0610	2.9e-3
cn	China	8,285	10,184	0.0212	2.9e-4
fr	France	211	167	0.0538	7.5e-3
gh	Ghana	5,648	26,697	0.0124	1.7e-3
ir	Iran	2,100	6,615	0.1339	3.0e-3
py	Paraguay	2,091	8,900	0.0368	4.1e-3
sg	Singapore	25,523	131,298	0.0474	4.0e-4
us	United States	22,392	75,794	0.0805	3.0e-4

between two vertices that have conflicting polarities. We ignore directions of both positive and negative links. Finally, we combine users from these eight countries into an undirected signed graph, denoted as myGamma.

Epinions. Epinions is a product review web site. Users can write subjective reviews about many different types of items, such as software, movies and music videos, etc. A trust network is defined among these Epinion users (Leskovec *et al.*, 2010). We download the network from the Stanford Large Network Dataset Collection.[2] We perform the same pre-processing similar to myGamma and we obtain another undirected trust network, denoted as Epinions.

The descriptive statistics of the two real networks are shown in Table 6.5. myGamma consists of 68,575 vertices and 293,327 links of which 5.5% are negative. Epinions consists of 131,828 vertices and 253,772 links of which about 1.8% are negative. To save space, Figure 6.21 only shows various power-law degree distributions of myGamma network. The Epinions network follows similar properties. The default parameter settings are $min\_size = 3$, $\epsilon = 1$, and $\delta = \frac{1}{3}$.

6.8.2 Performance Results

Performance by varying countries. We apply both *aMascot* and *rMascot* on the country specific networks to determine the elapsed time and the numbers of *MQAC*s for each network.

---

[2]http://snap.stanford.edu/data/soc-sign-epinions.html

Table 6.5: Descriptive statistics for myGamma and Epinions networks.

Data	# users	# edges	*ratio*⁻	Density
myGamma	68,575	293,328	0.0552	1.2e-4
Epinions	131,828	253,772	0.0185	2.9e-5

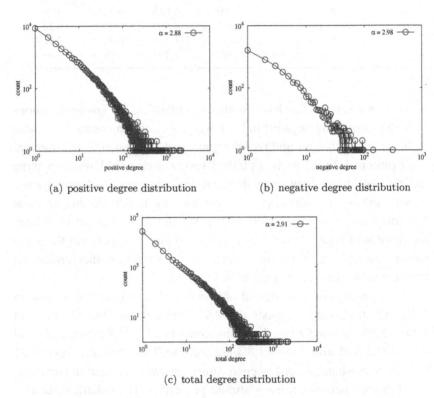

(a) positive degree distribution   (b) negative degree distribution

(c) total degree distribution

Fig. 6.21: Degree distribution of myGamma network.

Figure 6.22(a) illustrates the elapsed time for each country specific network. Among them, Singapore network requires the longest elapsed time, 1,000 and 6,000 seconds for *aQAC*s and *rQAC*s, respectively. This can be attributed to the large number of edges in the Singapore network (see Table 6.4). This results in more candidate graphs generated by the pruning stage. In the pruning stage, MASCOT therefore finds more candidate graphs. It takes longer time to process these candidate graphs

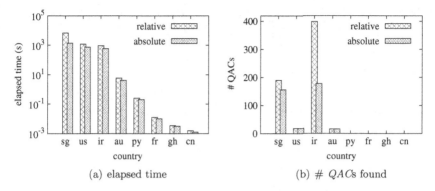

(a) elapsed time   (b) # *QAC*s found

Fig. 6.22: Performance by varying countries.

in the enumeration stage. The Iran network has few edges but a high proportion of negative links. It therefore requires more elapsed time.

Figure 6.22(b) shows the number of *MQAC*s found. Iran has the largest numbers of *aQAC*s and *rQAC*s. Again, this is due to the high proportion of negative links. This result is consistent with the earlier result shown in Figure 6.18.

Performance by varying *min_size* **on myGamma.** We apply both *aMascot* and *rMascot* on myGamma network by varying the parameters *min_size*, ϵ, and δ. Figures 6.23(a) and 6.23(c) show this elapsed time. The elapsed time generally decreases with larger *min_size* and small ϵ (or δ). Nevertheless, the elapsed time is much longer for these larger real networks. This is consistent with our earlier results on the synthetic graphs. Figures 6.23(b) and 6.23(d) show the number of *MQAC*s found. In summary, *aMascot* and *rMascot* take several hours to finish for *min_size* = 3, but much less time when *min_size* > 3.

In addition, we also compare MASCOT with the algorithm for detecting *DAC*s [Lo *et al.* (2011)] on myGamma when $\epsilon = 0$ or $\delta = 0$. Under these conditions, the *QAC* will also be a *DAC*. We show the results of our experiments in Figures 6.23(a)–6.23(d). From Figures 6.23(a) and 6.23(c), when *min_size* is large, both *aMascot* and *rMascot* are more efficient than the algorithm that mines *DAC*s. Figures 6.23(b) and 6.23(d) indicate that *aQAC* and *rQAC* help us to find more antagonistic communities due to their relaxed conditions. The results are consistent with our earlier results on the synthetic graph.

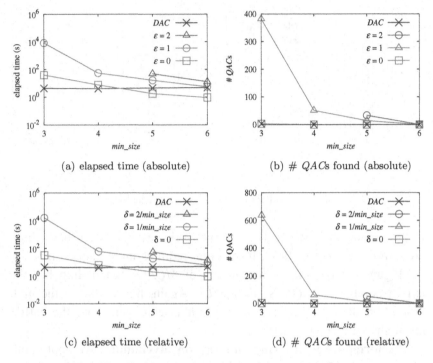

(a) elapsed time (absolute)   (b) # QACs found (absolute)

(c) elapsed time (relative)   (d) # QACs found (relative)

Fig. 6.23: Performance by varying *min_size* on myGamma.

Performance by varying *min_size* on Epinions. Figures 6.24(a) and 6.24(c) show the elapsed time by varying the parameters *min_size*, ϵ and δ on Epinions. Figures 6.24(b) and 6.24(d) show the number of *MQAC*s found. The observation is consistent with our earlier results on both the synthetic graphs and myGamma network.

Meanwhile, we compare MASCOT with the algorithm for detecting *DAC*s (Lo *et al.*, 2011) on Epinions when $\epsilon = 0$ or $\delta = 0$. We also show the results of our experiments in Figures 6.24(a)–6.24(d). From Figures 6.24(a) and 6.24(c), when *min_size* is large, *aMascot* and *rMascot* are more efficient than the algorithm that detects *DAC*s. From Figures 6.24(b) and 6.24(d), we find that *aQAC* and *rQAC* help us to find more antagonistic communities. The results are also consistent with our earlier results on the synthetic and myGamma networks.

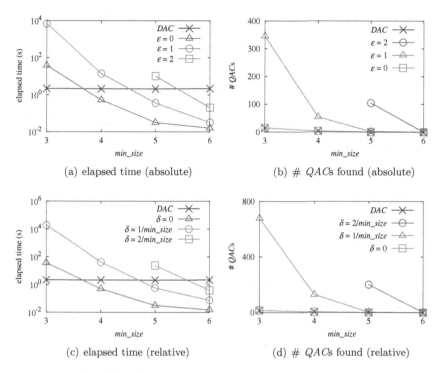

Fig. 6.24: Performance by varying *min_size* on Epinions.

6.8.3 Example Cases

For a better understanding of the effectiveness of MASCOT we now examine the actual QACs found in myGamma networks.

Cross-countries community. Most users link to the other users from the same country. We however would like to examine if any QACs exist between users from different countries. So as to obtain cross-country network for finding $MQAC$s, we combine users from Singapore, USA and Iran in various ways. As shown in Table 6.6, we cannot find any new absolute $MQAC$s by combining Singapore users with Iran users. When combining the users from the three countries, we found three additional absolute $MQAC$s ($355 - 156 - 178 - 18 = 3$) whose members are from different countries. These three absolute $MQAC$s are induced by the

Table 6.6: Statistics for detecting cross-countries *MQAC*s.

Countries	Absolute		Relative	
	# *MQAC*s	time (s)	# *MQAC*s	time (s)
sg	156	1,387.7	190	6,681.1
us	18	742.9	18	1,182.6
ir	178	597.9	399	930.5
sg+ir	334	1,594	589	7,089.3
sg+ir+us	355	2,318.3	610	8,271.8

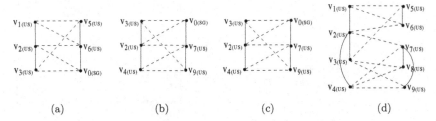

(a)　　　　　　(b)　　　　　　(c)　　　　　　(d)

Fig. 6.25: *QAC*s formed by users from different countries.

same Singapore user v_0 as shown in Figure 6.25. The same observation can be found for relative *MQAC*s.

6.8.4 *Predicting Polarity of Links*

We now want to determine if detecting *QAC* is helpful in predicting the sign of an individual edge. We employ supervised machine learning approach to classify if an individual edge inside a detected *QAC* is positive or negative.

Features. To build the classifier, we group a collection of features of edges from a *QAC* into three categories. Suppose that we are interested in predicting the sign of the edge from u to v. The first group of features is related to the degrees of u and v. Specifically, we use $deg^+(u)$, $deg^+(v)$, $deg^-(u)$, $deg^-(v)$, $deg(u)$, and $deg(v)$ to denote the number of positive neighbors, of u to v, the number of negative neighbors of u to v, and the total number of neighbors of u to v. The second group is the triad feature which is the set of count of triads involving edge (u, v).

We use $tri^+(u, v)$, $tri^-(u, v)$ and $tri^\pm(u, v)$ to denote the number of common positive neighbors, the number of common negative neighbors, and the number of users who have different kinds of relationships to u to v. The final type of feature is a community feature which is a binary feature. It is 1 if u to v come from the same sub-community of a *QAC* or the same community detected by maximizing modularity (following the algorithm described in Mucha *et al.* (2010)), otherwise 0.

Learning Methodology and Results. We built three sets of classifiers. One set is built based on degree feature and triad feature, except for the community feature, denoted as **N-C**. The second one is built based on degree feature, triad feature, and *QAC*-based community feature, denoted as **C_Q**. The final one is built based on degree feature, triad feature, and modularity-based community feature, denoted as **C_M**. Each set of classifiers consists of five classifiers: Naive Bayes, AD-tree, J48, Weka SVM, and logistic regression.

We randomly select 600 edges from our found *MQAC*s, which consist of 317 positive edges and 283 negative edges, on both myGamma and Epinions networks. We employ 10-fold cross-validation to evaluate the results. Table 6.7 illustrates precision, recall, and F-measure of the learning results on both myGamma and Epinions networks, where F-measure is computed as $\frac{2 \times \text{precision} \times \text{recall}}{\text{precision} + \text{recall}}$. We observe that the predicted results with the

Table 6.7: Accuracy for predicting signs of edges on myGamma and Epinions.

Data	Approach	Precision			Recall			F-measure		
		C_Q	C_M	N-C	C_Q	C_M	N-C	C_Q	C_M	N-C
myGamma	NaiveBayes	**0.978**	0.816	0.653	**0.979**	0.901	0.823	**0.978**	0.853	0.728
	ADTree	**0.992**	0.927	0.861	**0.986**	0.916	0.845	**0.989**	0.921	0.853
	J48	**0.987**	0.926	0.864	**0.994**	0.936	0.878	**0.990**	0.931	0.871
	SMO	**0.996**	0.922	0.848	**0.995**	0.940	0.885	**0.995**	0.931	0.866
	Logistic	**0.998**	0.918	0.838	**0.997**	0.933	0.868	**0.997**	0.925	.853
Epinions	NaiveBayes	**0.962**	0.838	0.713	**0.971**	0.862	0.753	**0.966**	0.849	0.732
	ADTree	**0.971**	0.898	0.824	**0.976**	0.894	0.812	**0.973**	0.896	0.818
	J48	**0.979**	0.920	0.861	**0.977**	0.910	0.843	**0.978**	0.915	0.852
	SMO	**0.982**	0.909	0.836	**0.980**	0.913	0.846	**0.981**	0.911	0.841
	Logistic	**0.991**	0.924	0.856	**0.987**	0.918	0.849	**0.989**	0.921	0.852

community feature outperform those without the community feature. Also, our *QAC*-based community feature outperforms the modularity-based community feature in predicting the polarities of links.

6.8.5 *Discussion: Coverage and Applicability*

Our goal is to identify strong local communities that fight among one another. In a typical network, nodes involved in these antagonistic communities are expected to be small in number — since otherwise there would be too many fights and the network might even crumble into multiple networks. Thus, by design, our antagonistic communities will not have high coverage. Most of the nodes in a typical network would not be part of any antagonistic community.

However, despite low coverage, antagonistic community mining still has a number of applications. Detecting antagonistic communities would help a network administrator to detect unwanted antagonism early and prevent it from spreading too much in the network. By detecting antagonistic communities, one can also study factors that lead to antagonism in a large network which will enrich existing studies in social science that have typically only analyzed small datasets. Antagonistic communities can also be helpful to predict link polarity, user preferences, product adoption, etc. Of course, the low coverage of antagonistic communities might limit their utility in these applications; however, for nodes that are covered by these antagonistic communities (which could still be a large number, e.g., thousands of nodes), the detected communities can help in these tasks — as shown in Section 6.8.4.

6.9 Conclusion

In this chapter, we detect dense sub-structures from a signed graph, called *quasi-antagonistic communities* (*QAC*s). An antagonistic community consists of two groups of users expressing positive relationships within each group but negative relationships across groups. Instead of requiring complete set of negative links across its groups, a *QAC* allows a small number of inter-group negative links to be missing. We propose an algorithm, MASCOT, to find all *MQAC*s. MASCOT consists of two stages: pruning and enumeration stages. Based on the properties of *QAC*, we propose four pruning rules to reduce the size of candidate graphs in the pruning stage. We use an enumeration tree to enumerate all *strongly connected subgraphs* in a top-down fashion in the second stage before they are used to construct $MQAC$s.

We also demonstrate that MASCOT achieves good recall, returning the QACs injected into synthetic graphs. And in the myGamma social network, a real world network, we observe that most QACs are among users from the same country. Finally, we find that detecting QACs is helpful to predict the sign of an individual edge from both myGamma and Epinions networks.

Chapter 7

Summary

7.1 Conclusions

In the era of big data, the advent of online social networks has been one of the most exciting events in this decade. Many social networks, such as Facebook, Twitter, Sina Weibo, Foursquare, and Flickr, etc., are extremely rich in content, and they typically contain a tremendous amount of content and linkage data which can be leveraged for mining. The linkage data is essentially the network structure which records the communications between users; the content data includes the text, image, and other multimedia data in the platforms.

The richness of the context of social networks provides unprecedented opportunities for the mining in the social networks. The mining of social networks is a rapidly growing and an interdisciplinary field at the crossroad of disparate disciplines deeply rooted in sociological theory, data science, statistics, and graph mining, etc. The fast-growing interests and intensifying need to harness social network data require research and the development of tools for finding insights from the social network data. There are two elementary kinds of data which are often mined in the context of social networks:

- **Network structure mining:** In the structural analysis, we construct analysis of the linkage behaviors of the networks to evaluate the network robustness and local communities in bipartite and signed networks. Such mining tasks provide a good overview of both the global and local evolution behaviors of the underlying networks.

165

- **Content-based mining:** Many social networks, such as Twitter and Foursquare, contain a tremendous amount of content which can be leveraged to improve the quality of data mining. To identify the user from the different social networks, combining content-based mining with structure-based mining provides more effective results.

7.2 Discussion of Future Directions

It is always difficult to determine which research direction is most important or will become more popular, especially in an area as fast evolving as the richness of the context of social networks. However, in this book we will make a few audacious statements about the future directions, without the hope of being completely correct, but reflecting some opinions we hope to be useful to the audiences.

- **Privacy in social networks:** With the proliferation of social networks, there has been increasing concern about the privacy of individuals participating in them. There are two scenarios for privacy in social networks. In the first scenario, an adversary is interested in learning the private information of an individual using publicly available social network data. In the second scenario, a data provider would like to release a social network data to researchers but preserve the privacy of individuals.
- **Link prediction:** Link prediction is an important task for analyzing social networks which also has many applications including, automatic web hyper-link creation, bioinformatics, personalized recommendation, etc. Although there exist a variety of techniques for link prediction, ranging from feature-based classification, matrix factorization, and graphical models, it is a challenging task due to the sparsity of social network data.
- **Social influence:** Social influence is the effect that people have upon the beliefs or behaviors of others. Social influence may be represented by peer pressure, persuasion, marketing, sales, and conformity. A natural question is how to model social influence by utilizing both the structural and content data.
- **Information cascading:** Information cascades are phenomena in which an action or idea becomes widely adopted due to the influence

of others, typically, neighbors in some networks. The diffusion of information and influence through a social network is greatly affected by the topology of the network. However, human interactions may be modeled with networks, and attributes of these networks often follow heavy-tailed distributions, i.e., power law distributions. Fitting heavy-tailed distributions is a very difficult task.

Bibliography

Abello, J., Resende, M. G. C., and Sudarsky, S. (2002). Massive quasi-clique detection, in *Latin American Theoretical Informatics Symposium*, pp. 598–612.

Alba, R. D. (1973). A graph-theoretic definition of a sociometric clique, *Journal of Mathematical Sociology* **3**, pp. 113–126.

Albert, R., Jeong, H., and Barabási, A. L. (2000). The internet's achilles' heel: Error and attack tolerance in complex networks, *Nature* **406**, pp. 378–382.

Alvarez-Hamelin, I., DallÁsta, L., Barrat, A., and Vespignani, A. (2008). K-core decomposition of internet graphs: hierarchies, self-similarity and measurement biases, *Networks and Heterogeneous Media* **3**, 2, pp. 371–393.

Alvey, I. (2011). Expander graph and property, Technique report, pp. 1–17.

Anchuri, P. and Magdon-Ismail, M. (2012). Communities and balance in signed networks: A spectral approach, in *ASONAM*, pp. 235–242.

Asur, S. and Huberman, B. A. (2010). Predicting the future with social media, in *Web Intelligence and Intelligent Agent Technology (WI-IAT)*, Vol. 1 (IEEE), pp. 492–499.

Balakrishnan, R. (2004). The energy of a graph, *Linear Algebra and its Applications* **387**, pp. 287–295.

Ball, B., Karrer, B., and Newman, M. E. J. (2011). An efficient and principled method for detecting communities in networks, *Physical Review E* **84**, pp. 36–103.

Ball, F., Mollison, D., and Scalia-Tomba, G. (1997). Epidemics with two levels of mixing, *The Annals of Applied Probability*, pp. 46–89.

Bansal, N., Blum, A., and Chawla, S. (2004). Correlation clustering, *Machine Learning* **56**, 1–3, pp. 89–113.

Beyene, Y., Faloutsos, M., Chau, P., and Faloutsos, C. (2008). The ebay graph: How do online auction users interact? in *Computer Communications Workshops Co-located with INFOCOM 2008*, pp. 13–18.

Bilenko, M. and Mooney, R. J. (2003). Adaptive duplicate detection using learnable string similarity measures, in *KDD*.

Blei, D. M., Ng, A. Y., and Jordan, M. I. (2003). Latent dirichlet allocation, *Journal of Machine Learning Research* **3**, pp. 993–1022.

Blondel, V. D., Guillaume, J.-L., Lambiotte, R., and Lefebvre, E. (2008). Fast unfolding of communities in large networks, *Journal of Statistical Mechanics: Theory and Experiment* **10**, pp. 1–12, doi:doi:10.1088/1742-5468/2008/10/P10008, http://doi.acm.org/10.1145/362342.362367.

Bobkov, S., Houdré, C., and Tetali, P. (2000). vertex isoperimetry and concentration, *Combinatorica* **20**, 2, pp. 153–172.

Bron, C. and Kerbosch, J. (1973). Algorithm 457: finding all cliques of an undirected graph, *Communications of the ACM* **16**, 9, pp. 575–577.

Bu, D., Zhao, Y., Cai, L., Xue, H., Zhu, X., Lu, H., Zhang, J., Sun, S., Ling, L., Zhang, N., Li, G., and Chen, R. (2003). Topological structure analysis of the protein-protein interaction network in budding yeast, *Nucleic Acids Research* **31**, 9, pp. 2443–2450.

Callaway, D. S., Newman, M. E., Strogatz, S. H., and Watts, D. J. (2000). Network robustness and fragility: Percolation on random graphs, *Physical Review Letters* **85**, 25, p. 5468.

Cartwright, D. and Harary, F. (1956). Structure balance: A generalization of heider's theory, *Psychological Review* **63**, 5, pp. 277–293.

Cavers, M., Fallat, S., and Kirkland, S. (2010). On the normalized laplacian energy and general randić index r-1 of graphs, *Linear Algebra and its Applications* **433**, 1, pp. 172–190.

Chaudhuri, S., Ganjam, K., Ganti, V., and Motwani, R. (2003). Robust and efficient fuzzy match for online data cleaning, in *SIGMOD*.

Cho, E., Myers, S. A., and Leskovec, J. (2011). Friendship and mobility: user movement in location-based social networks, in *Proceedings of the 17th ACM SIGKDD International Conference on Knowledge Discovery and Data Mining* (ACM), pp. 1082–1090.

Christen, P. (2012). A survey of indexing techniques for scalable record linkage and deduplication, *IEEE Transactions on Knowledge and Data Engineering* **24**, 9, pp. 1537–1555.

Chung, F. R. (1997). *Spectral Graph Theory*. American Mathematical Society, Providence, RI.

Cohen, R., Erez, K., Ben-Avraham, D., and Havlin, S. (2000). Resilience of the Internet to Random Breakdowns, *Physical Review Letters* **85**, 21, p. 4626.

Cucerzan, S. (2007). Large-scale named entity disambiguation based on wikipedia data, in *EMNLP*.

Dandekar, P. (2010). Analysis and generative model for trust networks, Technique report, pp. 1–5.

Day, J. and So, W. (2007). Singular value inequality and graph energy change, *Electronic Journal of Linear Algebra* **16**, pp. 291–299.

Day, J. and So, W. (2008). Graph energy change due to edge deletion, *Linear Algebra Application* **428**, pp. 2070–2078.

Dekker, A. H. and Colbert, B. D. (2004). Network robustness and graph topology, in *Proceedings of the 27th Australasian Conference on Computer Science-Volume 26* (Australian Computer Society, Inc.), pp. 359–368.

Donetti, L. and Munoz, M. A. (2004). Detecting network communities: a new systematic and efficient algorithm, *Journal of Statistical Mechanics: Theory and Experiment* **2004**, 10, pp. P10012(cond–mat/0404652).

Doreian, P. and Mrvar, A. (1996). A partitioning approach to structural balance, *Social Networks* **18**, 2, pp. 149–168.

DuVall, S. L., Kerberc, R. A., and Thomasa, A. (2010). Extending the fellegi–sunter probabilistic record linkage method for approximate field comparators, *Journal of Biomedical Informatics* **43**, 1.

Elmagarmid, A. K., Ipeirotis, P. G., and Verykios, V. S. (2007). Duplicate record detection: A survey, *IEEE TKDE* **19**, 1, pp. 1–16.

Eubank, S., Guclu, H., Kumar, V. A., Marathe, M. V., Srinivasan, A., Toroczkai, Z., and Wang, N. (2004). Modelling disease outbreaks in realistic urban social networks, *Nature* **429**, 6988, pp. 180–184.

Everett, M. (1982). Graph theoretic blockings, k-plexes and k-cutpoints, *Journal of Mathematical Sociology* **9**, pp. 75–84.

Fellegi, I. P. and Sunter, A. B. (1969). A theory for record linkage, *Journal of the American Statistical Association* **64**, 328.

Fiedler, M. (1973). Algebraic connectivity of graphs, *Czechoslovak Mathematical Journal* **23**, 2, pp. 298–305.

Gao, M., Lim, E., and Lo, D. (2013). *R*-energy for evaluating robustness of dynamic networks, in *Web Science 2013 (co-located with ECRC), WebSci '13*, Paris, France, May 2–4, 2013, pp. 89–98, doi:10.1145/2464464.2464486, http://doi.acm.org/10.1145/2464464.2464486.

Gao, M., Lim, E., Lo, D., and Prasetyo, P. K. (2016). On detecting maximal quasi antagonistic communities in signed graphs, *Data Min. Knowl. Discov.* **30**, 1, pp. 99–146, doi:10.1007/s10618-015-0405-2, https://doi.org/10.1007/s10618-015-0405-2.

Gao, M., Lim, E., Lo, D., Zhu, F., Prasetyo, P. K., and Zhou, A. (2015). CNL: collective network linkage across heterogeneous social platforms, in *2015 IEEE International Conference on Data Mining, ICDM*

2015, Atlantic City, NJ, USA, November 14–17, 2015, pp. 757–762, doi:10.1109/ICDM.2015.34, https://doi.org/10.1109/ICDM.2015.34.

Giatsidis, C., Thilikos, D. M., and Vazirgiannis, M. (2011). Evaluating cooperation in communities with the k-core structure, in *2011 International Conference on Advances in Social Networks Analysis and Mining*, pp. 87–93.

Girvan, M. and Newman, M. E. J. (2004). Finding and evaluating community structure in networks, *Physical Review E* **69**, p. 026113.

Goga, O., Lei, H., Parthasarathi, S. H. K., Friedland, G., Sommer, R., and Teixeira, R. (2013). Exploiting innocuous activity for correlating users across sites, in *WWW*, pp. 447–458.

Grannis, S. J., Overhage, J. M., and McDonald, C. J. (2002). Analysis of identifier performance using a deterministic linkage algorithm, in *AMIA*.

Groshaus, M. and Szwarcfiter, J. L. (2010). Biclique graphs and biclique matrices, *Journal of Graph Theory* **63**, 1, pp. 1–16.

Gutman, I. (1978). The energy of a graph, *BeT. Math.-Stai'ist. Sekt. FOTschnngsz. Gmz* **103**, pp. 1–22, doi:doi:10.1088/1742-5468/2008/10/P10008, http://doi.acm.org/10.1145/362342.362367.

Hasegawa, T. and Masuda, N. (2011). Robustness of networks against propagating attacks under vaccination strategies, *Journal of Statistical Mechanics: Theory and Experiment* **2011**, 09, p. P09014.

Heider, F. (1946). Attitudes and cognitive organization, *Journal of Psychology* **21**, pp. 107–112.

Heider, F. (2013). *The psychology of interpersonal relations* (Psychology Press).

Hoory, S., Linial, N., and Wigderson, A. (2006). Expander graphs and their applications, *Bulletin of the American Mathematical Society* **43**, 4, pp. 439–561.

Iofciu, T., Fankhauser, P., Abel, F., and Bischoff, K. (2011). Identifying users across social tagging systems, in *ICWSM*.

Jamakovic, A. and Van Mieghem, P. (2008). On the robustness of complex networks by using the algebraic connectivity, in *International Conference on Research in Networking* (Springer), pp. 183–194.

Jamali, M. and Abolhassani, H. (2006). Different aspects of social network analysis, in *Web Intelligence*, pp. 66–72.

Java, A., Song, X., Finin, T., and Tseng, B. (2007). Why we twitter: understanding microblogging usage and communities, in *Proceedings of the 9th WebKDD and 1st SNA-KDD 2007 workshop on Web mining and social network analysis* (ACM), pp. 56–65.

Johnson, D. S., Yannakakis, M., and Papadimitriou, C. H. (1988). On generating all maximal independent sets, *Information Processing Letters* **27**, 3, pp. 119–123.

Karrer, B. and Newman, M. E. J. (2011). Stochastic blockmodels and community structure in networks, *Physical Review E* **83**, p. 016107.

Kong, X., Zhang, J., and Yu, P. (2013). Inferring anchor links across heterogeneous social networks, in *CIKM*.

Koudas, N., Sarawagi, S., and Srivastava, D. (2006). Record linkage: similarity measures and algorithms, in *Proceedings of the 2006 ACM SIGMOD International Conference on Management of Data* (ACM), pp. 802–803.

Lacoste-Julien, S., Palla, K., Davies, A., Kasneci, G., Graepel, T., and Ghahramani, Z. (2013). Sigma: simple greedy matching for aligning large knowledge bases, in *SIGKDD*, pp. 572–580.

Leicht, E. A., Girvan, M., and Newman, M. E. J. (2006). Vertex similarity in networks, *Physical Review E* **73**, p. 026120.

Leskovec, J., Huttenlocher, D., and Kleinberg, J. (2010). Signed networks in social media, in *Proceedings of the SIGCHI Conference on Human Factors in Computing Systems* (ACM), pp. 1361–1370.

Leskovec, J., Kleinberg, J., and Faloutsos, C. (2005). Graphs over time: densification laws, shrinking diameters and possible explanations, in *Proceedings of the Eleventh ACM SIGKDD International Conference on Knowledge Discovery in Data Mining* (ACM), pp. 177–187.

Leskovec, J., Lang, K. J., Dasgupta, A., and Mahoney, M. W. (2009). Community structure in large networks: Natural cluster sizes and the absence of large well-defined clusters, *Internet Mathematics* **6**, 1, pp. 29–123.

Li, J., Sim, K., Liu, G., and Wong, L. (2008a). Maximal quasi-bicliques with balanced noise tolerance: Concepts and co-clustering applications, in *SIAM International Conference on Data Mining*, pp. 72–83.

Li, J., Sim, K., Liu, G., and Wong, L. (2008b). Maximal quasi-bicliques with balanced noise tolerance: Concepts and co-clustering applications, in *Proceedings of the SIAM International Conference on Data Mining, SDM 2008, April 24–26, 2008, Atlanta, Georgia, USA*, pp. 72–83, doi: 10.1137/1.9781611972788.7, https://doi.org/10.1137/1.9781611972788.7.

Liben-Nowell, D. and Kleinberg, J. (2007). The link-prediction problem for social networks, *Journal of the American Society for Information Science and Technology* **58**, 7, pp. 1019–1031.

Liu, G. and Wong, L. (2008). Effective pruning techniques for mining quasi-cliques, in *European Conference on Machine Learning and Knowledge Discovery in Databases*, pp. 33–49.

Liu, J., Zhang, F., Song, X., Song, Y.-I., Lin, C.-Y., and Hon, H.-W. (2013). What's in a name? an unsupervised approach to link users across communities, in *WSDM*.

Liu, S., Wang, S., Zhang, J., Zhu, F., and Krishnan, R. (2014). Hydra: Large-scale social identity linkage via heterogeneous behavior modeling, in *SIGMOD*.

Liu, X., Li, J., and Wang, L. (2008). Quasi-bicliques: Complexity and binding pairs, in *The 14th Annual International Computing and Combinatorics Conference*, pp. 255–264.

Lo, D., Surian, D., Prasetyo, P. K., Zhang, K., and Lim, E.-P. (2013). Mining direct antagonistic communities in signed social networks, *Information Processing Management* **49**, 4, pp. 773–791.

Lo, D., Surian, D., Zhang, K., and Lim, E.-P. (2011). Mining direct antagonistic communities in explicit trust networks, in *Proceedings of the 20th ACM International Conference on Information and Knowledge Management* (ACM), pp. 1013–1018.

Lu, C., Shuai, H., and Yu, P. S. (2014). Identifying your customers in social networks, in *CIKM*, pp. 391–400.

Luce, R. D. (1950). Connectivity and generalized cliques in sociometric group structure, *Psychometrika* **15**, pp. 169–190.

Luce, R. D. and Perry, A. D. (1949). A method of matrix analysis of group structure, *Psychometrika* **14**, 2, pp. 95–116.

Malliaros, F. D., Megalooikonomou, V., and Faloutsos, C. (2012). Fast robustness estimation in large social graphs: Communities and anomaly detection. in *SDM*, Vol. 12 (SIAM), pp. 942–953.

Mann, H. B. (1945). Nonparametric tests against trend, *Econometrica: Journal of the Econometric Society*, pp. 245–259.

Mishra, N., Ron, D., and Swaminathan, R. (2005). A new conceptual clustering framework, *Machine Learning* **56**, 1–3, pp. 115–151.

Mokken, R. J. (1979). Cliques, clubs and clans, *Quality and Quantity* **13**, pp. 161–173.

Moon, J. W. and Moser, L. (1965). On cliques in graphs, *Israel Journal of Mathematics* **3**, 1, pp. 23–28.

Mucha, P. J. and Porter, M. A. (2010). Communities in multislice voting networks, *Chaos* **20**, p. 041108, doi:doi:10.1088/1742-5468/2008/10/P10008, http://doi.acm.org/10.1145/362342.362367.

Mucha, P. J., Richardson, T., Macon, K., Porter, M. A., and Onnela, J.-P. (2010). Community structure in time-dependent, multiscale, and multiplex networks, *Science* **328**, 5980, pp. 876–878.

Narayanan, A. and Shmatikov, V. (2009). De-anonymizing social networks, in *S&P*, pp. 173–187.

P. J. Mucha, K. M. M. A. P., T. Richardson and Onnela, J.-P. (2010). Community structure in time-dependent, multiscale, and multiplex networks, *Science* **328**, pp. 876–878.

Palla, G., Derényi, I., Farkas, I., and Vicsek, T. (2005). Uncovering the overlapping community structure of complex networks in nature and society, *Nature* **435**, pp. 814–818.

Palmer, C. R. and Steffan, J. G. (2000). Generating network topologies that obey power laws, in *Global Telecommunications Conference, 2000. GLOBECOM'00. IEEE*, Vol. 1 (IEEE), pp. 434–438.

Ravikumar, P. and Cohen, W. W. (2004). A hierarchical graphical model for record linkage, in *UAI*.

Robbiano, M. and Jimenez, R. (2009). Applications of a theorem by ky fan in the theory of graph energy, *MATCH: Communications in Mathematical and in Computer Chemistry* **62**, pp. 537–552.

Ronhovde, P. and Nussinov, Z. (2009). Multiresolution community detection for megascale networks by information-based replica correlations, *Physics Review E Stat Nonlinear Soft Mattering Physics* **80**, p. 016109 19658776.

Roos, L. L. and Wajda, A. (1991). Record linkage strategies. part i: Estimating information and evaluating approaches, *Methods of Information in Medicine* **30**, 2.

Sadinle, M. and Fienberg, S. E. (2013). A generalized fellegi–sunter framework for multiple record linkage with application to homicide record systems, *arXiv:1205.3217v2* .

Scannapieco, M., Figotin, I., Bertino, E., and Elmagarmid, A. K. (2007). Privacy preserving schema and data matching, in *SIGMOD*.

Shen, Y. and Jin, H. (2014). Controllable information sharing for user accounts linkage across multiple online social networks, in *CIKM*, pp. 381–390.

Sim, K., Li, J., Gopalkrishnan, V., and Liu, G. (2006). Mining maximal quasi-bicliques to co-cluster stocks and financial ratios for value investment, in *Sixth International Conference on Data Mining (ICDM'06)* (IEEE), pp. 1059–1063.

Sim, K., Li, J., Gopalkrishnan, V., and Liu, G. (2009). Mining maximal quasi-bicliques: Novel algorithm and applications in the stock market and protein networks, *Statistical Analysis and Data Mining* **2**, 4, pp. 255–273, doi:10.1002/sam.10051, https://doi.org/10.1002/sam.10051.

Tarjan, R. E. (1972). Depth-first search and linear graph algorithms, *SIAM Journal on Computing* **1**, 2, pp. 146–160, doi:10.1145/362342.362367, http://doi.acm.org/10.1145/362342.362367.

Traag, V. A. and Bruggeman, J. (2009). Community detection in networks with positive and negative links, *Physical Review E* **80**, p. 036115, doi:10.1103/PhysRevE.80.036115, http://doi.acm.org/10.1145/362342.362367.

Wainwright, M. J. and Jordan, M. I. (2008). Graphical models, exponential families, and variational inference, *Foundations and Trends® in Machine Learning* **1**, 1–2, pp. 1–305.

Wasserman, S. and Faust, K. (1994). *Social Network Analysis: Methods and Applications* (Cambridge University Press).

Whang, S. E., Menestrina, D., Koutrika, G., Theobald, M., and Garcia-Molina, H. (2009). Entity resolution with iterative blocking, in *SIGMOD* (Lausanne, Switzerland).

Woodbury, G. (2002). *An Introduction to Statistics* (Cengage Learning).

Wu, C. J. (1983). On the convergence properties of the em algorithm, *The Annals of Statistics*, pp. 95–103.

Yakout, M., Elmagarmid, A. K., Elmeleegy, H., Ouzzani, M., and Qi, A. (2010). Behavior based record linkage, *PVLDB* **3**, 1, pp. 439–448.

Yan, C., Burleigh, J. G., and Eulenstein, O. (2005). Identifying optimal incomplete phylogenetic data sets from sequence databases, *Molecular Phylogenetics and Evolution* **35**, pp. 528–535.

Zafarani, R. and Liu, H. (2009). Connecting corresponding identities across communities, in *ICWSM*.

Zafarani, R. and Liu, H. (2013). Connecting users across social media sites: a behavioral-modeling approach, in *Proceedings of the 19th ACM SIGKDD International Conference on Knowledge Discovery and Data Mining* (ACM), pp. 41–49.

Zhang, H., Kan, M., Liu, Y., and Ma, S. (2014). Online social network profile linkage, in *AIRS*, pp. 197–208.

Zhang, K., Lo, D., and Lim, E.-P. (2010). Mining antagonistic communities from social networks, in *The 14th Pacific-Asia Conference on Knowledge Discovery and Data*, pp. 68–80.

Zhang, K., Lo, D., Lim, E.-P., and Prasetyo, P. K. (2013). Mining indirect antagonistic communities from social interactions, *Knowledge Information System* **35**, 3, pp. 553–583.

Zheng, W., Zou, L., Feng, Y., Chen, L., and Zhao, D. (2013). Efficient simrank-based similarity join over large graphs, *Proceedings of the VLDB Endowment* **6**, 7, pp. 493–504.

Zhou, B. (2010). More on energy and laplacian energy, *MATCH: Communications in Mathematical and in Computer Chemistry* **64**, pp. 75–84.

Zhou, B., Gutman, I., and Aleksic, T. (2008). A note on the laplacian energy of graphs, *MATCH: Communications in Mathematical and in Computer Chemistry* **60**, pp. 441–446.

Index

East China Normal University Scientific Reports
Subseries on Data Science and Engineering

Published (continued from page ii)

Printed in the United States
By Bookmasters